BROWNING AND THE FICTIONS OF IDENTITY

BROWNING AND THE FICTIONS OF IDENTITY

E. Warwick Slinn

BARNES & NOBLE BOOKS
TOTOWA, NEW JERSEY

© E. Warwick Slinn 1982

All rights reserved. No part of this publication may be
reproduced or transmitted, in any form or by any means,
without permission

First published in the U.S.A. 1982 by
BARNES & NOBLE BOOKS
81, Adams Drive, Totowa,
New Jersey, 07512
ISBN 0–389–20273–8

Printed in Hong Kong

Library of Congress Cataloging in Publication Data

Slinn, E. Warwick, 1943–
  Browning and the fictions of identity.

  Includes bibliographical references and index.
  1. Browning, Robert, 1812–1889—Criticism and
interpretation.   2. Browning, Robert, 1812–1889—
Characters.   3. Characters and characteristics in
literature.   4. Identity (Psychology) in literature.
I. Title.
PR4239.S5   1982   821'.8   81–24197
ISBN 0–389–20273–8   AACR2

For my parents
Eric and Vera Slinn

Contents

Preface

This book arises out of the simple aim of explaining what Browning meant by 'action in character', although the explanation itself is at times not so simple. Browning seems to me to be a psychological dramatist who used monologues to explore man as the product of a self-reflexive use of language. Consequently my concern is with the nature of the histrionic in his poetry, with the way characters are engaged in verbal acts which dramatise themselves, and with the way Browning considers the multiplicity and complexity of human personality, re-examining its nature and suggesting the richness of its possibilities. The dramatic monologue is a form which almost invariably raises questions about personality and reflexive consciousness, so that dramatic tension becomes focused on conflicts about self-conception. In this, Browning is clearly a nineteenth-century subjectivist, although at the same time he challenges a Romantic epistemology which assumed a continuity between experience and reality. 'To reach reality we must first repudiate experience', wrote Lévi-Strauss in *Tristes Tropiques* (New York, 1961), and Browning questions the truth of experience by exposing the ironies of conceptualising and the fallibility of his speakers. He emphasises therefore not the speaker's subject, but the speaker *as* subject. While the raw data of material existence remains, its meaning may be transformed or redefined through linguistic artifice. For Browning this process is the ironic drama which lies at the heart of all human consciousness; and it means that in his poetry the elusive suggestiveness of metaphoric and aesthetic language coincides with the ambiguous reality of a subject-determined view of experience.

Life for Browning's characters is frequently a tightrope walk between a multitudinousness which threatens to fragment and diffuse experience on the one hand, and the self-determined fiction of a controlled solipsism on the other. As they confront the impositions of a world which would absorb them into its own shaping processes, speakers are engaged in defence of their very existence as individuals, and they often retaliate through acts of verbal aggression which attempt instead to subsume the world into *their* web of understanding. Out of this flux emerge the fictions which form a basis for personal identity.

In examining Browning's portrayal of this drama, I have endeavoured to avoid the inflexibility of clinical terms taken from modern personality theory. While this may at times seem to lead to some imprecision of analysis, his poetry is not a system, and I think the variety of his characterisation and form requires an openness of approach which avoids the restrictions of distinguishing between conflict models, fulfilment models or consistency models. I have used terms, then, mainly in their ordinary dictionary sense: personality as 'being a person', 'having the distinctiveness of an individual human being'; and identity as 'oneness', 'the quality of being the same', 'the condition of being a specified person', or simply 'individuality'. It should also be noted that I use the words 'illusion' and 'fiction' descriptively, not pejoratively.

All quotations from Browning's poetry, except where otherwise indicated, are taken from *Browning: Poetical Works 1833–1864*, ed. Ian Jack (London: Oxford University Press, 1970). Two of my chapters have been previously published: Chapter 6 appeared in *Journal of English Literary History*, 42 (1975), 651–68 (I have made minor revisions to this article), and Chapter 2 appeared under the title ' "God a Tame Confederate": the Reader's Dual Vision in *Pippa Passes*', in *University of Toronto Quarterly*, 45 (1976), 158–73. I am grateful to the Johns Hopkins University Press and to the University of Toronto Press for permission to reprint these essays here.

My first serious attempt to work on Browning was supervised by Professor William E. Fredeman at the University of British Columbia and if it were not for his disciplined training and friendly encouragement I might never have proceeded this far. It will be apparent from other acknowledgements in the course of my discussion that the main influences on my reading of Browning have been the writings of Robert Langbaum, Morse Peckham and Isobel Armstrong, and in a real sense this study could not have been written without their work. For their publications, and for those by Roma King and David Shaw, I am indeed grateful. I am indebted also to the Victorian Studies Centre at Leicester University for providing me with facilities that greatly assisted my writing, and to Massey University for granting me sabbatical leave and therefore the time to write. Finally I should mention Suzann Olsson, since her refusal to indulge my tantrums or to sustain my petty triumphs combined with her scepticism to provoke a ruefully acknowledged impetus towards continued explanation.

E.W.S.

Massey University
New Zealand
May 1980

1 The Repudiation of Experience

Browning's poetry is characteristically mimetic, not in the older pre-Romantic sense of imitating an order believed to be inherent in the natural world, some independently created reality, but in the more modern sense of imitating ways of thinking and speaking about the world. With the growing nineteenth-century anxiety about publicly shared beliefs, poets were increasingly required to examine the assumptions underlying their creativity, in particular the relationship between poetic language and its referential world. Shelley, for instance, argues that poetry could free men from the tyrannical deception of a contingent and habitual reality: poetry, he says, 'creates anew the universe, after it has been annihilated in our minds by the recurrence of impressions blunted by reiteration'.[1] Shelley still refers to 'the' universe, a transcendent realm which sense impressions veil or distort and which it is the poet's task to reveal, but by suggesting that poetic language may order the world, he detaches words from a strict representation of things and raises the possibility of a new series of created realities, a different order of mimetic art characterised by metaphoric relationships rather than direct imitation. Clearly such a possibility questions the objective nature of reality, and in this context poetry becomes increasingly dramatic, shifting the emphasis from what is perceived to the processes of perception, from the structure of an external world to the structuring powers of individual minds.[2]

The natural conclusion to this trend is solipsism, and later in the century Pater's description of the mind imprisoned within its own impressions of the world follows naturally from Coleridge's proposition that 'we receive but what we give, / And in our life alone does nature live', from Shelley, and from Tennyson's decision to dream his dream and 'hold it true'.[3] However, the dangers of such a self-circumscribed view were recognised from the start: in Shelley's 'Alastor', for instance, where the hero-poet dies through pursuing

an illusion which he fails to realise is of his own making, a projection
of his own ideal soul-image (or anima). While the world of
phenomena may be transcended through metaphoric intensity or
transformed through imaginative colouration, and while Shelley in
particular seeks a metaphoric truth based on the reality of poetic
images (as he does in 'Mont Blanc'), there are always physical and
temporal limits to mortal life. What ultimately constitutes reality or
represents truth may be questionable, but sensations and phenomena remain.

The existence of a common physical world is rarely, if ever,
denied by nineteenth-century writers, though what is certainly in
doubt is the meaning and value of that world. Novels, through
temporal and historical structures, tend to reinforce the awareness
of this shared reality, while much of the poetry, particularly that
influenced by the combined traditions of lyric verse and philosophical idealism, tends to view the conventional world sceptically, as
something to be experienced, but as fundamentally a deception. In
many cases this scepticism is an expression of what Northrop Frye
calls 'the Darwinian crisis of separating mythological from natural
time',[4] as it is, for example, in *In Memoriam*: 'The hills are shadows
and they flow . . .'. Here for Tennyson the perspective of an
evolutionary time-scale undermines a common-sense tangibility.
With Browning, however, scepticism takes on a different form. Less
concerned with the differentiation of mythological time-scales, he is
more ready, like the novelists, to work within the limits of a natural
existence. 'For it is with this world', he says in the *Essay on Shelley*,
'that we shall always have to concern ourselves: the world is not to
be learned and thrown aside, but reverted to and relearned.'[5]
Consequently, his poems contain a profusion of sensory detail which
affirms a physical actuality and the monologues generally define a
temporal experience through imitating one of the most basic of
historical events, the conversation. As we are thrust into a series of
loose-structured, transient-natured forms of one-sided talk, we are
invariably confronted with the contingency of event and shape-
lessness of life which we associate with everyday reality; it is perhaps
the superficial formlessness and illusion of spontaneity in the
monologues which most suggests their contiguity with life, their
slice-of-life realism. In this way Browning's poetic devices can be
seen to reinforce mimetic rather than aesthetic elements: unity is to
be found in the realities of characterisation rather than in abstract
rhetorical patterns, and hence, for example, the couplets in 'My

Last Duchess' function as an aspect of the Duke's psychological need to impose order and control on his life.

Yet Browning is a poet and elements of stanza structure and rhyme, or more usually alliteration and rhythm, impress a formal composure on his personae's conversations which is at odds with their verisimilitude. Dukes do not normally speak in couplets, nor painters in blank verse. Although these devices are unobtrusive they are nonetheless present, and poetic artifice in Browning's work becomes more than an aspect of aesthetic form which is suppressed through suspension of disbelief. It infuses itself into the subject-matter, introducing a level of patterning which draws attention not so much to an overall design as to the characters' manipulation of what they say. The Duke of Ferrara compulsively seeks to control his language as well as his wives, so that even his frankness is a contrivance. Such an act is a measure of the imposition of his will on the world and while it does not make him a poet (except in terms of the truism that any fictional character who speaks in verse is a poet), it can be seen to follow from the possibilities for creative language raised by Shelley. While characteristically retaining the impression of a tactile world and physically or historically existing personae, Browning's poetry illustrates the way the meaning of that world is shaped and patterned by those who perceive it.

We are faced with the paradox that Browning's mimetic method challenges the assumptions of mimetic art. Through dramatising men thinking about the world, he imitates a process which transforms, and it is more often than not the transformation which is paraded as reality by his characters. The elements of artifice in a Browning monologue mean therefore that it is less a slice-of-life than a contrived representation of the contrivance in human reality. Browning employs the illusion of a person speaking in order to suggest the illusion in human understanding; the point is not only to portray experience but also to question it, and he does this by indicating the linguistic artifice which underlies all speech. While spontaneous conversation reinforces a commonplace realism, there is another paradoxical sense in which it undermines the illusion: in the way that temporal progression is constantly impeded. Elliptical, heavily parenthetical sentences tend to break the pattern of normal syntax with its forward movement and so divert attention from ends to process. Consequently, although there is a necessary overall temporal dimension to a monologue, since that is how everyday experience occurs, there is little intermediate temporal or narrative impetus, and in so far as syntactic interruption draws attention to itself, it minimises the referential aspect of the language, depreciating the realism and encouraging a sense of the artifice in human expression. Consider, for example, these two excerpts:

> This grew; I gave commands;
> Then all smiles stopped together.
>   ('My Last Duchess', ll. 45–6)

> I might have done it for you. So it seems:
> Perhaps not. All is as God over-rules.
> Besides, incentives come from the soul's self;
> The rest avail not.   ('Andrea del Sarto', ll. 132–5)

In each of these quite different examples the narrative referential dimension is less the point than the syntactical structuring. What the 'commands' were or whether God really 'over-rules' is hardly relevant. Rather than building an impetus which leads to future resolution as in more conventional mimetic narratives, these passages narrow the focus onto the present shaping. In the Duke's case the focus is on the stark simplicity of completed action and his fastidious satisfaction in the implied causality between 'I gave' and 'stopped together'. The structure of the statement contains both the Duke's arrangement of events and the continuing importance of that arrangement. Andrea's example focuses on an oscillation between assertiveness and withdrawal, confidence and uncertainty, with the passage barely surviving a dissolution into syntactic distress. The imitative function remains, or else we could not recognise the poems for the acts of human conception which they are, but the mimesis is functional rather than substantive. That is to say, the mimetic dimension is not the poem's achievement or aim, but it is inextricable from the monologue's dramatic action. Not the referential reality but the process by which it is produced is important. Browning went on in the *Essay on Shelley* to say that 'spiritual comprehension may be infinitely subtilised, but the raw material it operates upon, must remain' (p. 67). This statement may seem to assert the primacy of matter, but he is saying rather that he is not a solipsist, and he invariably indicates the physical limits to that fictional world: Don Juan's touch, Fra Lippo Lippi's 'sportive ladies' and Caliban's mud. The phenomenal experience or raw material is there in the texture of the verse, but it is contained within an actively perceiving consciousness. Each poem focuses on 'spiritual comprehension', on the act of consciousness which absorbs that material, shaping it, recreating it, or as Browning says, relearning it.

Browning's scepticism, then, emerges not in the form of an evolutionary crisis over duration, but in terms of a profound doubt about the function of human perception:

> Only, at heart's utmost joy and triumph, terror
>> Sudden turns the blood to ice: a chill wind disencharms
> All the late enchantment! What if all be error –
>> If the halo irised round my head were, Love, thine arms?
>>> ('Epilogue' to *Ferishtah's Fancies*)

This doubt anticipates what Frye has described as man's third, more modern crisis: 'the distinguishing of the ordinary waking consciousness of external reality from the creative and transforming aspects of the mind'. And Browning's poetry often resolves itself, thematically and functionally, into the characteristic question of this crisis – 'the question of the relation of ordinary life, which begins at birth and ends at death and is lived within the ordinary categories of linear time and extended space, to other possible perspectives on that life which our various creative powers reveal'.[6] Through the dramatisation of continually various conceptual forms, acts of consciousness, Browning's creativity explores the possibilities and limits of a humanly shaped realism. In other words, he dramatises an ambiguous experience which relies on assumptions about a common phenomenal world and at the same time challenges those assumptions; he affirms a reality and yet embodies it in a formulation which is a demonstrable contrivance.

I wish to stress this suggestion that the 'experience' in Browning's poetry is fundamentally ambiguous, since criticism has tended to assume for the monologues a conventionally mimetic contiguity between poem and world which is rather part of their illusion, the questioned reality, than their intended function. Robert Langbaum's study, *The Poetry of Experience*, probably the best and certainly the most influential criticism on Browning in recent decades, establishes the conditions for ambiguous experience, but still treats Browning's poetry in terms of the more positive aspects of a literary form which is designed to overcome an ontological dualism. In Langbaum's view nineteenth- and twentieth-century literature is defined by its response to 'the legacy of the Enlightenment', a world in which fact is separated from value, where 'fact is measurable quantity' and 'value is man-made and illusory'.[7] It is a split between the physical world's intractable existence and man's perceiving intelligence, between actuality and interpretation, object (world) and subject (self). The Romantics attempted to resolve the dilemma by asserting the primacy of personal experience and by exploiting the power of imaginative recreation in order to affirm an empirically established truth. Value and reality are to be found through subjective commitment and not through abstract analysis. 'It is *matter* which is the abstraction, the mere theoretical concept derived from an analysis of experience; whereas "the life of things" is what we perceive at the moment when experience is immediate and unanalysed' (p. 22). The result is a radical alteration of what is fact – for Blake 'the object not in itself but as perceived, is the concrete fact' (p. 22) – and a poetry, epitomised by the dramatic monologue, which is based upon 'the deliberate disequilibrium between experience and idea' (p. 35).

For Browning the poetry undoubtedly does make 'its statement not as an idea but as an experience from which one or more ideas can be abstracted as problematical rationalizations' (pp. 35–6), but I would argue that Langbaum's emphasis on this disequilibrium between experience and idea needs to be redefined as an emphasis upon a disequilibrium within experience itself. Given their focus on individual perception, the Romantic poets tend to assume a continuity between experience and reality, a tacit phenomenology, and this assumption leads to a method of understanding which seeks a close identification of object and perceiving subject. The 'ultimate reality' of an object is therefore, in Langbaum's explanation, 'its organic connection . . . with the observer' (p. 42). But to reach such an end requires 'an act of imaginative projection', where 'the act of knowing organically requires that we imbue the object with life, finding in it the counterpart of our own consciousness' (p. 25), and in this reciprocal process there lurks the incipient solipsism which I referred to earlier. In an understanding established through this method there is always a potential irony in the recognition of its inherent self-reflection. Langbaum stresses the potential discrepancy or disequilibrium between immediate experience and its subsequent analysis, but he does not stress sufficiently this irony within the act of experience itself, since for most of Browning's characters experience is an active involvement of consciousness with sensation. As long as the Romantics avoid the basis of their organic identification, the subterfuge of imaginative projection, they are able to affirm the validity of their perception. They do this positively of course by asserting the value of imagination and its fusing power. But with Browning the subterfuge is more usually exposed than affirmed. Unlike Shelley, who revealed the hero-poet's self-deception in 'Alastor' by filtering the action through a narrative voice, Browning instead employs irony (the now commonplace 'unconscious irony' of the dramatic monologue) to undermine his characters and so break the bond of identification. Thus he builds into his poems a challenge to the assumed continuity between experience and reality.

In emphasising the validity of personal experience the Romantics relied also on another assumption about the existence and coherence of the consciousness-centred subject which is implicit in such experience. Any revelation or insight achieved through sympathetic identification could be trusted, because personally verified, in a way that abstract principle could not. Sometimes the nature of the event is obscure ('Was it a vision or a waking dream?'), but at least there was an experience, something happened, and 'as an experience, the illumination is undeniably valid' (Langbaum, p. 26). In so far as individual perception is 'a' reality this may be true, but again the irony in Browning's poetry questions or at least severely limits the application of this validity.[8] In the terms which Langbaum posits as an essentially Romantic position, any claim to a broadly applicable empirical validity is always potentially ironic because self-generating. Among others in recent decades, Norman Holland has pointed out how science now acknowledges the role of the subject, or observer, in human knowledge. Psychologists of cognition and perception, he says, 'have shown over and over again in a variety of contexts that perception is a constructive act'.[9] Irony functions in Browning's poetry to do the same thing: in undermining the conceptual authority of the speaker in a monologue, irony emphasises his fallibility, his role as subject. Ultimately Browning's legacy from his early mentor Shelley is not the authority of imagination, but a scepticism which although seeming at times to return him to an Enlightenment dualism, anticipates the more modern view that perception and conceptualising are barely separable.[10]

Browning's irony implies a repudiation of the validity of experience similar to that which led structuralists such as Lévi-Strauss to reject existentialism and phenomenology for making false assumptions about reality. However, whereas the structuralist aim was scientific, to overcome the subject-determined error of perspective, Browning still works within the Romantic framework of individual perception: all the individual has is what seems to be his own experience:

> What if all's appearance?
> Is not outside seeming
>   Real as substance inside?
> Both are facts, so leave me dreaming.
>
> ('Flute-Music, With an Accompaniment')

It has been frequently said that Browning developed the dramatic monologue as a means of escaping from the inherited condition of Romantic subjectivity, as an attempt to achieve an objectivity denied his Romantic predecessors. But Browning uses his personae to dramatise subjectivity, not to avoid it. If, as Langbaum says, 'the speaker directs his address outward in order to address himself, and makes an objective discovery in order to discover himself' (p. 200), then this is an entirely subjective process because caught in its own circularity. In so far as the characters attempt to interpret their world they become trapped in their own hermeneutic circle and far from coming to know themselves through self-objectification, as Langbaum claims (p. 25), they show through unconscious irony that they attain only the illusion of objectivity. Langbaum also suggests that 'the meaning of the dramatic monologue is what the speaker comes to perceive', but he immediately adds the qualification that 'the thing he comes to perceive is something more than the sum of what he sees or thinks' (p. 207). Here, however, Langbaum seems to confuse the speaker's perception with the reader's, for whatever is more than the speaker sees or thinks is not articulated by him and cannot be said to be part of his conscious perception. The reader may observe this transcendent truth, but for the speaker it must be beyond consciousness and more usually for him nothing new is learned. There may be glimpses of insight, such as Cleon's recognition of the paradoxes in human awareness or the Bishop of St Praxad's realisation that he will get only gritstone for his tomb, but invariably they are revealed to be prisoners of their own subjectivity, just as Cleon is trapped by pride and the Bishop reverts to his triumph with the mistress whom Gandolf envied. Even in 'Saul', where David's suppression of his own identity in his concern for Saul's needs may suggest an objective experience, the revelation of divine love is entirely subjective in that it emerges as a projection from David's own feelings. Neither the minimisation of irony nor David's self-denial makes the poem any the less an act of subjective consciousness; it is even more so because it is a recreation after the event.

What of the poet's detachment from his personae? If his irony reveals his characters' deceptions, then the implication is that he stands aloof from their turmoil, detached and therefore objective. But this view is ambiguous. Philip Drew is perhaps right to say that 'Browning's objectivity consists . . . in his presentation of a character without reference to himself'.[11] But in a strict sense an objective product is one detached from its author's emotional ethos, and while Browning's personal comments are removed from the monologues irony still reveals his feelings, clearly making the poems not objective. To regard Browning as a satirist who indicates his own attitudes, as Drew also does, is a contradiction of the view that he wrote monologues in order to be objective. Ultimately, all objectivity is an illusion because of the very irony which it apparently rests on. Irony may enforce the author's detachment from his work, but at the same time it is the sign of his involvement in the shaping.

Nor is the reader's detachment which is wrought by irony any guarantee of objectivity. Any form which depends for its central effects on what the speaker fails to observe, on its essential incompletion, clearly depends on the reader's active involvement. Such a commitment may result in immense satisfaction as the character is beaten at his own game, but this position of superiority, often an inextricable aspect of ironic detection, is only achieved through being a participant, through engaging in some measure in a process of mind and emotion entirely analogous to that of the protagonist. To recognise irony it is necessary to retain a sense of identity separate from the speaker (as Nabokov liked to observe, only 'minor readers' identify with the hero),[12] but to the extent that our own feelings and rationalisations are involved in discriminating among the hero's, we too are absorbed in a subjective process. The reader's subjectivity in this context may also be related to what is a widespread view in structuralist theory: that critical interpretation is the superimposing of one layer of language upon another.[13] The effect of this view is to blur the distinctions between literature and criticism, each being simply a different mode of language, a different level of meaning, and for the dramatic monologue this proposition helps to explain the close and active relationship between poem and reader. The nature of the form requires the reader to make an interpretation of what is overtly another interpretation – the speaker's view of himself and his world – and the result of this interaction is both an illusory depth of reality and an illusory objectivity in the reader's level of action. However, while ironic detachment is not the same as a scientific detachment which minimises the distortions of personal feeling, irony does draw attention to the processes of subjectivity, making them conscious in the mind of the reader. Through irony, Browning's monologues may be said to produce the same effect that is found in novels which acknowledge their own artifice, such as *Tristram Shandy*, Flann O'Brien's *At Swim Two Birds* or Nabokov's *Pale Fire*, where the reader is drawn directly into the process of creating fictions and making worlds. Engagement with this process is for the reader a potential means of escape from other people's fictions: by observing the irony which shows others to be snared by their own pre-conceived pattern, he may be able to avoid a similar trap. But in this Browning's poetry is heuristic rather than didactic. Recognition of the irony in 'Cleon', for instance, does not require that we become a Christian, only that we know about Christianity. We do not escape from subjectivity, then, by reading Browning's poetry, but we may gain a perspective on it.

Earlier twentieth-century emphasis on objectivity in poetry and the attitudes it engendered are perhaps no longer an issue; yet for a while they asserted considerable influence against nineteenth-century poetry and so may be held responsible for certain false impressions about the limits of poetic activity. Whatever value Eliot's 'objective correlative' has had, for example, in explaining the function of certain kinds of imagery, it has also fostered the illusion of a necessary objectivity. Emotion, Eliot says, can only be expressed in art through

> a set of objects, a situation, a chain of events which shall be the formula of that *particular* emotion; such that when the external facts, which must terminate in sensory experience, are given, the emotion is immediately evoked . . . this is precisely what is deficient in *Hamlet*. Hamlet (the man) is dominated by an emotion which is inexpressible, because it is in *excess* of the facts as they appear.[14]

Not only does this conception rely on a continuity between experience (feeling and sensation) and reality (objects), it also assumes a necessary correlation between sensation and consciousness. Of course Eliot seeks a synthesis of idealism and reality and the objectification of emotion, to avoid in an artistic context the mere assertion of unmotivated feeling, and so does Browning; but Browning is also aware that objectification may at the same time falsify, and the dramatic quality of his poetry often rests instead on a deliberate disjunction between sensation and consciousness, which is to do with psychological verisimilitude rather than a philosophical antithesis. This disjunction, or disequilibrium, is often revealed by the differences between images of external objects or perhaps simple narration, which are bound by spatial and temporal order and represent sensory perception, and metaphor, syntactic manipulation or structures of argument, which are not bound by spatio-temporal continuity and indicate the more complex actions and reactions of consciousness, whether in terms of memory, imagination or simply mind.

It is a disjunction which also characterises *Hamlet*. Hamlet is not dominated by an excess of emotion which is inexpressible, as Eliot claimed, but by the complexities of a subjective consciousness which renders all perception, and therefore action, doubtful. He is amazed, for instance, by the way an actor can suit his actions to a mere fiction ('his whole function suiting/With forms to his conceit', II.ii.566–7), whereas he, with far more motive and 'cue for passion', can only unpack his heart 'with words' (II.ii.597). But if an actor can combine words and action in a fiction, there is no guarantee of truth in the mere conjunction of word and deed. Hamlet's dilemma suggests that only through intentional action is integrity preserved, but to consider intention is to invoke immediately the problem of determining reality in the face of uncertain perception. Hamlet is confounded by puns, images, ambiguities, by the enormous possibilities in the relationships between thought and action, sensation and awareness. He proposes to do something ('About, my brains') and so organises a fiction (perhaps the only way to test reality), and his predicament anticipates the ironies of a more recent playing upon the restraints of consciousness in *Waiting for Godot*. Until we reach the more intricate self-consciousness of Bishop Blougram, Guido Franceschini or Don Juan, Browning's characters are generally less aware of potential deceptions than Hamlet, but an emphasis on process and the role of the subject in the monologues means that we are faced essentially with similar problems, with the operations of consciousness.

In 'Porphyria's Lover' it is the very objectivity of the narrative which is a startling illusion. The situation and the chain of events are carefully presented by the lover, but instead of becoming the formula for his emotion or the ratification of his deed, his set of facts reveals to the reader the dissociation between actuality (the events of his sweetheart's arrival and death) and the action of his consciousness (his dehumanisation of the girl into an accumulation of attributes). The regularity of the verse reinforces his control over the retelling, the fastidiousness of his calm, and the conjunctive phrase 'and yet' indicates the one disturbing element in his equanimity. In the last line ('And yet God has not said a word!'), Browning builds a finely poised ambiguity which captures both the speaker's confidence in his objectivity (he states only what has happened: God has indeed not spoken) and his growing uncertainty about God's silence (conveyed by the turn in 'and yet'). Browning provides neither speaker nor reader with an external judge, leaving only the speaker's reconstruction of events: the imposition of his solipsistic consciousness on the world.

The absence of overt moral comment does not make the poem amoral. In the monologues, we observe and are absorbed into the process of the speaker creating meaning, ourselves creating meaning in turn, translating his language into the language of our own interpretation. But we should also keep in mind the judgement involved, considering subjectivity not so much in terms of self-indulgence or relativism, as in terms of the responsibility that accompanies any making of meaning. Otherwise interpretation will be merely idiosyncratic. By this I do not mean that the reader becomes engrossed in determining moral culpability, to which so much Browning criticism has been reduced; nor do I mean that judgement is the point of the poems. Many critics seem to have lost sight of the way moral assessment tends to be either very easy or very difficult. Philip Drew, perhaps the main proponent of moral judgement, admits this variation, from monologues where Browning's attitude is unmistakable to those where the speaker cannot with certainty be placed, and Drew also accepts that in 'complex' monologues, 'we are not expected simply to condemn or sanctify the speaker' (Drew, p. 21). Nevertheless, he maintains, we are always required to judge the speaker's morality. My point is that in neither case can the reader's judgement be the point of the poem: when moral assessment is obvious it is superfluous – we hardly read 'My Last Duchess' simply to decide the Duke was wrong to murder his wife – and when it is not obvious the struggle to assess either becomes intertwined with other matters, as Drew hints, thereby losing its primacy, or it is futile, merely one more link in a long chain of critical disagreement. If, as is sometimes claimed, the monologues solicit an interest in 'the dangerous edge of things', to borrow Bishop Blougram's tightrope image, then the excitement lies in watching breathlessly the performance, in the suspense about success or failure, rather than in the success or failure itself – which in tightrope-walking is fairly obvious. As Blougram says of the performers, 'one step aside, / They're classed and done with' (ll. 400–1): with judgement there is dismissal. Moral irregularity is conducive to the excitement of the poems, and to the importance of perspective which all commentators note, but moral judgement for the reader is subordinate to a more general process of discrimination. Even in the difficult works, Drew argues, 'the monologue itself has involved us so deeply in the speaker's subject that we can make up our own minds about that, and then compare our position with the speaker's' (p. 21). But my view of experience in Browning's poetry brings me to a fundamental disagreement here: we are not involved in the speaker's subject, but in the speaker *as* subject. Consequently, making up our minds about the speaker's topic is also a subordinate task, part of a more central involvement in the whole process of his self-construction, part of the reader's absorption into the argumentative process, into the more unifying task of discerning relationships between perspectives and determining the limits of human ingenuity.

The subtleties of these processes of discrimination are indicated fully by Browning in *Fifine at the Fair*, for example when Don Juan considers how the value of drama depends on the way it is a deliberate lie: 'To feign, means – to have grace / And so get gratitude!' (LXXXV). But the illusion must be regarded as such; if we mistake the actor's 'false for true, one minute', all enjoyment and admiration is gone. This exercise of perception among truth and illusion parallels for Juan the same discernment which is required amidst the appearances and plays of life; it requires considerable mental agility to sustain, but it is essential to observing the paradoxical truths which are all that are available to men within the conditions of subjectivity – histrionic truth and the truth in falsehood. Through openly flaunting verbal artifice and a flirtation both literal and metaphoric with illusion, Don Juan illustrates the full perplexity of consciousness, the way experience may be characterised as a pageant, or how sensation may be transformed into a parade of the mind's imaginings. Browning's poems thus continue to explore, with varying degrees of awareness, the often ambiguous interrelationships between reality and contrivance, promoting often difficult distinctions between, in Frye's phrase, ordinary consciousness of external reality and transforming aspects of the mind. Browning's monologues are not a form to attain objectivity but a form to draw attention to subjectivity, to the ambiguity of language in forming experience. The reader is not so much outside the poem as inside it, caught in a dynamic interaction of three perspectives – poet, persona and reader – which is held together through the essentially ironic nexus of subjective processes.

This emphasis on irony does not deny at all the more positive aspects of sympathetic response, whether in reader or poet – the recognition, for instance, of a deeply felt need for love, belief and joy. Nevertheless, what endures in Browning's work is a vital scepticism about human experience which emerges simply and consistently as a dramatic strategy. In manipulating the personae of those whom he invents, Browning seems to have realised that almost any individual may manipulate his own persona, with or without being aware of doing so. As a consequence it is not so much the poet's act of dramatisation which the reader confronts as the characters' acts of dramatising themselves. In one respect self-dramatisation simply means that Browning's characters are to be seen making their own masks, as Betty Flowers has already observed, following Morse Peckham and with reference to Jung's theory that all men develop a persona or mask at the interface between self and society.[15] But the issue goes deeper, hinting in its subtleties of self-consciousness at the basic dynamics of self-generation, at problems of identity, freedom and psychological inertia; in short, self-dramatisation is the basic ploy in a drama of self-conception. It is what makes Browning a dramatist, focusing attention on the fundamental aspects of personality and rendering his art characteristically histrionic.

From Romantic individuality on into the increasingly dramatic poetry of the nineteenth and twentieth centuries, the dramatic monologue plays an important part in the complex refinement of self-consciousness. It can be seen in retrospect as an ideal form for representing the individual's simultaneous straining for self-expression and effort to view himself realistically. In the attempt to persuade an auditor, there is a reciprocal process which means that the speaker in a monologue demonstrates a deeply felt desire for both self-definition and self-understanding, and it was the brilliance of Langbaum's book to establish this kind of dual purposiveness. Langbaum suggests, for example, the implicit self-detachment in the monologuist himself:

> The thing we sense as we read the dramatic monologue, the thing that accounts for the peculiar effect which is the starting-point of our whole discussion of the form, is that the speaker has one foot inside the poem and one foot outside, that even as he engages in the action he is as much a spectator as we are (p. 204).

There is a good illustration of this effect in Andrea del Sarto's well-known description of himself in terms of 'sober pleasant Fiesole':

> There's the bell clinking from the chapel-top;
> That length of convent-wall across the way
> Holds the trees safer, huddled more inside;
> The last monk leaves the garden; days decrease,
> And autumn grows, autumn in everything.
> Eh? the whole seems to fall into shape
> As if I saw alike my work and self
> And all that I was born to be and do,
> A twilight-piece. (ll. 41–9)

The images imply the safe, protective and therefore dull retreat which Fiesole has become for Andrea, and he exploits in his favour a melancholy irony in that autumnal growth inevitably hastens winter death, but the crucial phrase 'as if' indicates his self-consciousness, the separation of the speaking self and the described self. As long as he can say the scene is 'as if' he saw himself 'a twilight-piece', Andrea maintains a detachment from his description which hints at another self which is not, or would not be, part of the 'autumn in everything'. He thus remains a spectator while being a participant, as Langbaum suggests, and the description of Fiesole as a proposed image or dramatisation *is* Andrea only in so far as he identifies with it; it represents only one perspective on himself, one which is naturally suited to his need for Lucrezia's sympathy.

But we need to go beyond the spectator image to the sense of a more penetrating refinement of dramatic conflict, or else the impression will be left that Browning's psychology is one of a simple distinction between public and private selves. This view is what is indicated of course if we stop with the construction of a Jungian persona – each character creates a public mask and watches himself as he does so.[16] Jung's theory of personality and individuation process are more complex affairs, however, and the whole advent of psychoanalysis has undermined the nineteenth-century sense of personality, at least as it is represented in literature, as something fixed, a discrete, opaque entity. We are well used now to the idea of a multifaceted self and the older concept can already be seen dissolving with Browning. In the extract above from 'Andrea del Sarto', for instance, Andrea maintains a passive separation from his surroundings by suggesting the difference between what happens out there, where everything 'seems to fall into shape' without his aid, and his internal perception, what he 'saw'. An external agency absorbs him into the 'twilight-piece', something which happens *to* him rather than something he initiates himself, and this location of cause within the world is part of Andrea's attempt to avoid responsibility for what he regards as his own failure. What torments him is his awareness of this passivity and his apparent inability to overcome it. The conflict generated deep within him by the tension between passive, not responsible, and active, possibly failing, selves underlies his fluctuating expressiveness throughout. In the Fiesole passage he does not even actively dramatise himself, taking up an image which is available ready-made, in effect merely blending with the landscape, and later, when he does provide his own metaphor, he still portrays himself as incapable of escape from enclosure:

> And I'm the weak-eyed bat no sun should tempt
> Out of the grange whose four walls make his world.
>
> (ll. 169–70)

As an image of blindness it is obviously appropriate, for it is Andrea's lack of vision or inspiration which makes his art less than Raphael's and Michelangelo's. Yet Andrea's self-knowledge is still not the point, since the reader is able to observe that this knowledge acts as a justification of inaction and is therefore crippling. In the impulse to retain control over his life and assert his self-respect, Andrea finally claims that he chooses his fate, but choice is an illusion for him; rather he conforms to an image which reinforces his timidity, predetermining his failure to act with any initiative. The dramatic subtlety of the poem lies in this ironic circularity: Andrea's self-image prevents a choice of action, or his inability to choose action predetermines his selection of self-image. His consciousness is thus caught between a passive self and the now dim prospect of an actively creative self, and in order to maintain some sense of identity he resorts to a necessary fiction, the histrionic pose of choice with its implicit impression of self-command.

Generally Browning retains the sense of a separately existing and distinctive individual (at least in the monologues which have named characters), and his tactile imagery reinforces the impression of his characters' physical presence, but in examples such as this he suggests a growing awareness of the multiple dimensions of personality. It is in the dynamics of self-dramatisation that such a breakdown begins, since they reveal the potentially ironic gap between self-expression and self-understanding; they hint at distinctions between various facets of consciousness (a 'dramatised' self implies another or 'real' self which does the dramatising) and suggest the snares of ambiguous consequences: a dramatic projection may be a means of self-realisation, merely a conveniently designed fiction, or a mixture of both, the endless configurations of a rationalised identity. In all this there is the essential disjunction in experience to which I have been constantly alluding; the character himself may not always be aware of it, but it provides the impetus for what Browning referred to as 'action in character'. Emerging from an age clearly subject to insecurities about personal identity – perhaps epitomised in *In Memoriam* – this disjunction seems characteristic of Browning's use of the monologue.

In my view the dramatic monologue is a form which almost invariably focuses on 'the nature of personality and perception'. Alan Sinfield, while accepting this as a direction in which longer examples of the form move, says it would be an exaggeration to argue 'that a poem like "My Last Duchess" is less about the Renaissance, marriage, pride, insecurity and aestheticism than about the nature of personality and perception'.[17] Certainly 'My Last Duchess' is about those topics, but they are themes generated from the shaping of personality and determined by the limits of perception which are dramatised in the poem. As Philip Drew observes, Browning 'gives the most exhaustive treatment in nineteenth-century verse of . . . one of the great ontological problems, that of the status of the personality of the individual' (Drew, p. 283), and in this there is no intrinsic difference between short and long monologues, only a matter of degree and complexity. Through the strategy of self-dramatisation Browning's dramatic action becomes one with his mimetic method. As his characters are caught in the struggle of expressing their desires, shaping their world through persuading their listeners, they are simultaneously caught in the internal conflicts associated with self-consciousness and making their own image; therefore the process of thinking about the world is concomitant with the essentially histrionic act of self-conception.

This is to view the characters in the monologues as indeed actors. They are to be seen, as Morse Peckham was the first to emphasise, as actors who are 'self-conceived, self-defined and self-deceived'.[18] The perception of man as actor is of course the characteristic metaphor of all drama, but in suggesting this metaphor in poetry, in a more privately experienced form than the theatre, Browning is able to exploit the increased potential for psychological subtlety in the more intimate method. The inherent isolationism of one person speaking, for instance, reinforces the intensively circumscribed, some might say almost claustrophobic, focus of action within an individual mind, and the ironies which expose the speaker's fallibility, his role as subject (both as perceiving agent and object of perception) point to the reciprocal action of consciousness. What is at first glance, in Peckham's definition, a solipsistic circle, is more often an hermeneutic one, where the characters are both inspired by the possibilities and trapped by the inadequacies, or ironies, of their efforts to interpret their life.

While each character is seen at one moment in terms of a particular state of mind, he is also caught in a complex of interrelationships which broaden the focus, as he is seen to exist in relation to his motives, both conscious and unconscious, to his past and future, and to the social milieu, usually represented by the auditor who is present, but often by others who figure prominently in his life; always, however, since physical action is minimal, this maze of interaction is a verbal affair and so exists entirely within the framework of the character's relationship with his dramatised self. The maze of relationships is the poem's and the character's world of action: he both acts within it and at the same time creates it through his acting. If there is any sense of the infinite within the finite in Browning's poetry, once a favourite description of his aims, it is not a transcendence of limits but an ever-continuing regress into the mechanisms of a single moment in human consciousness. In this regress too, and in the always implicit drama metaphor is

Browning's essential scepticism, since the dramatised propositions which represent the characters' beliefs allow Browning to provide another perspective on life without separating it from the process which shaped it, to propose hypotheses without removing them from the creative act which gave them meaning. This is the condition of experience as defined within his dramatic method, his art of the histrionic, and it is as if Shelley's concluding question to 'Mont Blanc' lingers on deep within Browning's mind:

> And what were thou, and earth, and stars, and sea,
> If to the human mind's imaginings
> Silence and solitude were vacancy?

2 'God a tame confederate': Irony in *Pippa Passes*

The literary problems associated with impersonal narration are now well known, and the extensive arguments which have developed about such works as *A Portrait of the Artist* or *The Turn of the Screw* should make changing interpretations of *Pippa Passes* less surprising. This experimental work, with its hybrid elements of picaresque, stage play and monologue,[1] and its varied tonal qualities from the opening lyrical splendour to Bluphocks' cynical doggerel, demands of its reader the same balancing of sympathetic involvement and ironic judgement as leads to so much of the ambiguity in modern literature. The difficulty of interpretation, however, is not just that caused by the disequilibrium between sympathy and judgement which has been the subject of debate about dramatic monologues;[2] the problem also involves the role of illusion in defining identity and a dramatic method which uses irony as a means of unity. Structurally, Browning brings together two essentially different approaches, the expressive and the mimetic, or the lyric and the dramatic, juxtaposing the single vision of an isolated mind with the multiple views of the social world. It has always been recognised that this method causes a problem in unity, but what has not been so obvious is the nature of the ironic vision which Browning provides for his reader.

In the absence of any clearly defined authorial figure the burden of unity has fallen upon Pippa herself, since the whole is circumscribed by her monologues. This focusing on her thoughts, however, has meant the drama was read as a parable about a moral universe supervised by God, and the variety of perspectives has thus been distorted. Rather, the structure of *Pippa Passes* emphasises the multitudinousness of life, which is more the raw material for irony than for theological optimism. As usual in Browning, abstract themes are intimately related to men's hopes and fears, their obsessions and assumptions; ideas are only given meaning by their

human context, so that the possibility of irony is admitted in almost
any circumstance. The context in this instance is hidden from
Pippa, yet is seen by the reader – the stock situation for dramatic
irony – and it produces not only the ironic contrasts of a world about
which Pippa is ignorant, but also alternative conceptions of human
behaviour. In this respect, consider these seldom noticed lines by
Phene when she describes the smile of the students who have tricked
Jules into marrying her:

> That hateful smirk of boundless self-conceit
> Which seems to take possession of the world
> And make of God a tame confederate,
> Purveyor to their appetites.[3]   (II. 158–61)

These lines not only counter Pippa's innocent vision, they over-
shadow the play, applying in varied degree to each episode and
encompassing even Pippa herself. Phene provides both a parallel
and a contrast to Pippa, being a girl of similar age,[4] though with a
clearly different experience of life. Phene, who has seen the realities
of jealousy and vanity, has seen how men 'make of God a tame
confederate', whereas Pippa, largely ignorant of human duplicity,
accepts the declaration of her New-year's hymn that 'each only as
God wills/Can work' (Intr.193–4). The experienced observe the
crabbed realities of human conceit, while the innocent accept a
more hopeful prospect, though, ironically, even Pippa unknowingly
condemns all human action to a deterministic charade.

It is a mistake, I believe, to regard Pippa's view or the philosophy
of her New year's hymn as representative of Browning's attitude in
this work. In context the theme of Pippa's hymn, that all men are
God's puppets, is ironic, since the play then presents the appearance
of free egos in a deterministic universe – a point frequently missed by
those who read the hymn as Browning's concluding message. The
latter, more theologically positive view is given its most sophisticated defence by Eleanor (Glen) Cook, who concludes that the
theme of the narrative is 'the irony of God's ways when regarded
from man's point of view'.[5] This interpretation, however, presup-
poses that the reader is placed in a position to see God's ways from
God's point of view, which can be accepted in the sense that the
reader sees all that happens at Asolo. But in that case who represents
man's point of view which 'regards' the irony? The reader sees the
discrepancies, not Pippa, and no-one else in the play is in a position

to perceive 'the deeper irony' which 'is due to the difference
between the theme of Pippa's New Year's hymn and the common
opinion that there are greater and lesser events and greater and
lesser men'.[6] In Browning's presentation of events only the reader
can observe such a distinction and if, as Mrs Cook implies, the
reader's view is to correspond to God's view, then God becomes an
observer of his own ironies. In Mrs Cook's interpretation there can
be no irony for God, only a 'fitness of things', a providential design,
and yet the overall view Browning provides in the play is the
reader's, who is always an observer of irony, and the only design
the reader can see is one where Pippa is the victim of irony. Perhaps
the *hymn* is meant to represent God's attitude, or to indicate it without
dramatising Him. If so, the hymn is not sufficiently imposing to
counter the irony in the remainder of the work. In *Paradise Lost*
Milton shows the lost paradise to be tragic in human terms, but
comic in divine terms, in the sense that all events move inexorably
towards redemption and a culmination in heavenly grace. There
the reader is able to experience both the tragedy, through Adam's
and Eve's sense of loss, and the comedy, through God's plan in Book
III and Michael's revelations to Adam in Books XI and XII. In *Pippa
Passes* the reader is not provided with a corresponding experience of
a divine purpose untouched by irony to offset the experience of an
ironic world, with or without providence. My quarrel with Mrs
Cook, then, is that she does not allow for the effects of Browning's
structure. At most the reader's vision is raised to a level which
enables him to imitate God's view; at the least, and more
realistically, God's view remains outside the play, something
mysterious, though hinted at in Pippa's hymn. In either case, unless
the reader ignores most of his experience in reading the work,
particularly his participation in Pippa's predicament, I cannot see
how to avoid the conclusion that God is an ironist who regards the
victims of his ironies with some equanimity.

Irony frequently requires a pattern to establish its presence and
determining the implications of that pattern is often difficult:
whether it indicates simply the author's control over his irony, or his
intention to reflect a providential plan which may be discerned in
all life. To point out that in *Pippa Passes* God becomes an ironist is
not therefore to deny that Browning may intend us to perceive the
evidence for a divine artificer, but it is to suggest that the God
indicated has ambiguous qualities, and certainly to argue that the
play's philosophy is not orthodox Christian doctrine. The issue is

further complicated of course by the effects of Pippa's songs on
the other protagonists, by Pippa's character and whether it affects
the authority of the hymn, and by any ironies surrounding the
conception that all are God's 'puppets'.[7]

If it is true, as has generally been accepted, that Pippa radically
changes the lives of those who hear her, and if she is to inherit her
rightful property, the play would have to be regarded as demonstrating providential fulfilment (in literary effect a rather
insipid poetic justice). However, even if only the concluding actions
are considered in each of the four main episodes, there are varying
degrees of ambiguity. Clearly Luigi leaves Asolo intent on as-
sassinating the Austrian emperor, and Jules intends to marry Phene
and take her to some new romantic spot, though the place itself is
vague (II.306). In the case of Sebald and Ottima it is widely
assumed that they commit suicide, but it does not seem to me clear
that they do, or necessarily that they will. Certainly they con-
template the act, but when does Sebald do it? The obvious point is
when he says, 'I, having done my deed, pay too its price!' (I.269). If
so, what is to be made of Ottima's following speech when she tries
desperately to stop him, attempting to soothe his passion in
motherly solicitude ('Lean on my breast – not as a breast'), and
particularly of her final words ('There, there, both deaths
presently!'), which, if we read 'presently' in the modern sense, imply
that she is successful in getting Sebald to postpone the event?
Another way is to interpret the repeated 'there' as referring to her
stabbing herself, and to take 'presently' in its archaic sense, but this
is awkward, at odds with the punctuation, and discordant with her
consolatory tone in the immediately preceding phrases. Also
Sebald's final images of 'waters/Loosened to smother up some
ghastly pit' and of 'whirls from a black fiery sea!' (I.280–2) function
more effectively if their metaphoric evocation of a disintegrating
consciousness is emphasised (death to self, whether or not to life),
rather than the macabre sensationalism of a literal wound.
Browning leaves the physical resolution uncertain and in doing so
dramatises more convincingly what we all know is his main
interest – 'action in character'. The Monsignor's concluding action
is perhaps more crucial in its effect upon larger interpretations, since
it is usually assumed that he will give his brother's estate to Pippa.
However, Browning leaves open another possibility, that the
Monsignor, by gagging the Intendant, will achieve two other aims:
to silence the villain, preventing his publication of the true facts

about the fortune, and to give the money to the Church – his wish
from the outset. Neither conclusion is supported by evidence which
Browning could easily have supplied, as he does for instance in the
case of Luigi (IV.ii.44–50), and consequently the Monsignor's
actions with regard to the estate are left deliberately unresolved.

Reflection about the morality of each response to Pippa's songs
discloses yet further ambiguity. Sebald's guilt is more a concern for
his own honour than for the crime itself; Jules's generosity in
marrying Phene is undercut by his enthusiasm for re-making her in
his own image; Luigi's patriotism is marred by his desire for
personal fame as a revolutionary; and the Monsignor is prompted
by his imminent death and so by his need to die with a clean record.[8]
Also, as Roma King has noted, Pippa does not introduce any new
idea to the actors: 'Sebald feels guilt, Jules aspires to the ideal, Luigi
feels compelled to kill the Austrian emperor, the Monsignor
recognizes moral obligation, *before* Pippa makes her appearance'.[9]
The degree and nature of Pippa's influence, then, are seriously
questionable.

Faced with this realisation that Browning obscures both the
morality and the action of each conclusion, Jacob Korg and Roma
King argue that Pippa's contribution is to enable the characters to
make any choice at all, thus saving them from 'the damnation of
spiritual and moral non-existence'.[10] Certainly the characters hope
to establish their existence, seeking to impose their personality on
the world in some form or other, but I cannot agree with Professor
Korg that they have a restored capacity 'for exercising enlightened
free will and moral judgement' (p. 9). Browning focuses attention
on the moment of response, and therefore on the psychology of each
incident, and in doing so he portrays the way people act according
to self-conceived illusions about themselves. In attempts to make the
illusion real, they manifest what they dimly perceive, consciously or
unconsciously, to be their true self. Pippa's songs may expedite
choice, but that decision is predetermined in each case by the
listener's idealism about himself. Far from introducing them to a
new dimension, Pippa reminds them of their selfhood. Her songs,
occurring at four moments of stress in the play, are the points at
which self and world merge, and her perspective is assimilated by
each character in such a way as to show his deepest desire, his real
self. Thus Browning shows how men 'take possession of the world' by
absorbing it into their personality; at the same time God is assumed

to applaud, and therefore to be a confederate, a 'purveyor' to their 'appetites'.

Sebald responds to Pippa by taking up the line 'God's in his heaven'. Initially this seems a simple reaction, expressing his recognition of a moral universe and of his own sinfulness, but Sebald's sense of morality is a complex self-conscious affair. His emotions are triggered throughout by a growing awareness of his inability to sustain the image of a romantic lover. It is not the deed itself which disturbs him (''T is not the crime's sake – I'd commit ten crimes / Greater, to have this crime wiped out, undone!'; 1.152– 3), but the perception that this particular act was not consistent with his romance idealism – 'Do lovers in romances sin that way?' (1.142). He intended to act in accord with the ideal of the noble lover, committing a crime for some grand passion, and he had anticipated living afterwards with the exquisite sensation of justified sin, convinced that he would at least have 'lived' (1.137–9). He thought of being 'Magnificent in sin' (1.218), with even 'a recompense in guilt' (1.135), but instead of a reckless lover he realises he has been merely a 'cut-throat' (1.57). The deed is the same but the word is different, and Sebald's self-consciousness about words (he frequently plays with words and their application to events) dramatises his disillusionment as he tries desperately to confront his responsibility:

> Let us throw off
> This mask: how do you bear yourself? Let's out
> With all of it. . . .
> Best speak again and yet again of it,
> Till words cease to be more than words. 'His blood',
> For instance – let those two words mean 'His blood'
> And nothing more.   (1.40–6)

These two passages are apparently ambivalent. On the one hand he wants to cease pretending, to remove the mask and so admit the crime; on the other to remove the associative meaning of words, reducing them to a clinical valueless referent which would avoid moral judgement. The oscillation hints at an inner struggle to resolve his doubts about the murder, but the second statement is also consciously ironic, indicating a deeper awareness of the reality he cannot avoid. This reality, however, is not that he has sinned; it is that he has failed to make real his illusory ideal of himself. What he has to face is not so much a God of judgement as his disillusionment, his own knowledge that he is not after all a lover but a cut-throat. His final speech, with its images of a disintegrating consciousness, follows naturally this awareness that his personality has not conformed with his ideal view of it, and the obliteration of consciousness is the more important conclusion than physical death. However, his punishment, reinforced with the idea of a cosmic judge, God in his heaven, becomes also a means of regaining self-respect, and the excessive quality of his emotional impulses throughout indicates the strength of his appetite for self-definition. His response to Ottima's seductiveness, for example (1.202–6), is as intensive as his earlier outbursts about her euphemisms – 'the devil take such cant!' (1.52). It is consistent, then, that he should finally turn on Ottima with such vehemence, verbally stripping away the mask which has enslaved him (1.239–48), since this very violence is the only assertion of self which he can now make with any resolution. When he says that he knows 'which is the better . . . /Of vice or virtue, purity or lust' (1.264–5), he admits a larger morality, but when he continues to say he is 'proud to feel/Such torments', he shows that his guilt and self-judgement are now as much a manifestation of himself and of his need to think well of himself as his pursuit of romance idealism had been earlier. 'God's in his heaven' has become a refrain for Sebald which reinforces his disillusionment and allows him at the same time to forge a new self out of the torment of guilt. His final rage is rather a remaking of his idealism about himself than a perception of morality therefore. He has not so much recognised the morality of God's world as the immorality of his own selfhood, and Pippa's song has functioned to confirm him in his self-centred guilt, enabling him to assert his identity in some more ideal way than as a courtly subordinate to Ottima, his 'spirit's arbitress'. Sebald's version of the Christian paradox of self-abnegation is to destroy his consciousness in order to define it.

As an artist Jules's play with illusion is the most overt in the drama. Significantly, the essence of his aesthetic vision is an idealising process which pursues the 'human archetype' (II.86); the world's objects provide him merely with 'suggestive germs' which his imagination can transform, attempting to 'better nature's birth by means of art' (II.84). In his eyes such activity is the quest for ideal beauty, and mastery over his medium the means of embodying the illusion, but it also means that the world is grist for his aesthetic manipulation rather than something in itself. Marble to him is like a creature from the earth's depths where 'itself breeds itself' (II.103) before it is refined by him; he takes possession of the world by idealising it in art. This tendency of mind, and the arrogance with which he expresses it, is what the students wished to exploit – to lure him on by his own impulses until he was forced to confront the discrepancy between his fanciful conceit and the tangible reality. What they failed to anticipate was the strength of the impulse and his ability to transfer his idealising from art into life.

His opening speech to Phene displays some facile raptures over spiritual union with his beloved. Superficially, he seems anxious to enjoy a relationship in which she figures equally ('You by me,/And I by you'), but it is the tangible form of his fancies that he worships (II.22–4), and he is attracted by the images she provides ('This length of hair and lustrous front; they turn/Like an entire flower upward'), not by any regard for her personality. As with Sebald, it is the excessiveness of his trite romanticising which reveals the energetic thrust of being, the effort to establish his selfhood by, paradoxically, changing himself into her (II.8–10). At this point he believes her to be a realisation of his aesthetic ideal; therefore to become absorbed in her form is to define himself through being linked with the illusion. When he discovers the reality about her, that the ideal is tainted, the affront to his dignity calls for revenge, until Pippa's song raises a new possibility. Phene's soul is unformed. Having created in marble, he now sees an opportunity to create in flesh, and the aesthetic quest for ideal beauty is transformed into the even more ambitious quest to mould a personality. This transference of aims emerges from Jules's adaptation of the song to his own circumstances by inverting its point of view – a page whose love for his Queen is frustrated by having no opportunity to demonstrate it. It is as the counterpart of the Queen that Jules considers his role; in other words, he instinctively places himself in the position of power able to help the page-boy, Phene. He has to admit that Phene is not the actuality of aesthetic beauty that he thought she was, but instead of a ready-made ideal, she now provides the raw material for him to transform. What has changed is his perception of Phene; what has not changed is his desire to embody idealised beauty or the illusion that he cherishes about his creative authority. He also longs 'to hear/God's voice plain' as he first heard it before the students' laughter broke in (II.303–5), but before Phene's recitation the voice was his own, prompting his search for archetypes. Consequently he

makes God the echo of his own voice, and believes he now has God's
sanction for taking possession of Phene by creating her soul as he had
earlier possessed the world through aesthetic transformation.

Luigi also alters the details of the song which he overhears in
order to apply the story to his own circumstances. The song's direct
application is to remind him of his ideal of a just king, but he extends
its significance beyond this. The Python in the song which did not
dare assault the King becomes, for Luigi, an image for the King of
Austria, an object of fear which other men are afraid to attack. This
patriotic characterisation may be justified, but when he adds that
'God would crown' for slaying the Python, and asks if crowns are
'yet to be won' once he overcomes his weakness (III.227–8), he
reveals a more fundamental motivation – the desire for reward and
fame. He, too, has appropriated God in his quest: ' 'T is God's voice
calls: how could I stay?' (III.229). Perhaps he sees the song as divine
inspiration: the reader can also see it as reinforcing his original
purpose, though he still fails to articulate any reasons for his
intention. Earlier, on being unable to explain to his mother the
necessity for the assassination he could only 'boast' the superiority of
'feeling'. His is the arrogant cry of an inarticulate idealist who
claims to 'understand' without being able to 'restate the matter'
(III.142–3). It is an attitude that may well produce irony, since such
reliance on emotion means that he is spared the embarrassment of
analysing his motives too carefully in case a desire for personal
aggrandisement might be masquerading as patriotic 'feeling'.
Luigi's exuberant assurance that will not doubt itself (III.58) is more
the result of youthful self-importance than founded on knowledge
about the political situation. When he walks among the townsfolk,
he is troubled because Italy is suffering, but when his thoughts are
prompted by 'Dreams long forgotten' (III.47), there is a hint of the
role which illusion plays and of the manner in which his incipient
sense of identity encompasses both the world and the heavens:

> And earth seems in a truce with me, and heaven
> Accords with me, all things suspend their strife,
> The very cicala laughs 'There goes he, and there!'
> 'Feast him, the time is short; he is on his way
> 'For the world's sake: feast him this once, our friend!'
>
> (III.49–53)

This flattering speech which he assigns to the cicala clearly indicates his reflexive view of things, and his possession of the world is complete when he excitedly anticipates telling the dead about earth's sunsets and rainbows: 'Gone are they, but I have them in my soul!' (III.83). Similarly, his approach to death is appropriately careless, but just a little too eager ('The dying is best part of it'; III.65), hinting at the way it is for him the climax of his illusory ideal of self-fulfilment; and the culmination of his account of the assassination is not the celebration of Italy's freedom, but his being joined by other heroic revolutionaries (III.121–3). The ease with which a selfish man may embrace the world within his self-love and so exalt himself in the name of the world is realised by his mother (III.124–9), but once Pippa's song reminds Luigi of his cause she cannot dissuade him. Pippa's song simply reinforces his idealism about himself enabling him to aggrandise himself while believing he serves God and nation.

The male protagonists so far have evinced the excessive language of over-anxious personalities, revealing thereby their inner natures, but in the fourth episode the Monsignor's cool intellectualism is more difficult to penetrate. His confident urbanity stems partly from his rank in the Church, which in itself gains him the respect if not the awe of people around him, and partly from his smoothly controlled speech, which enables him to handle the Intendant's taunts with bland assurance. But Browning is already gaining mastery over the apparently innocuous phrase with ironic undertones and there are still hints of the Monsignor's covert impulses. When dissociating himself from his family's wickedness, for example, he says his 'glory springs from another source', where 'glory' suggests the pride in his identification with the Church. He discloses not only a desire to redeem 'whole centuries of sin' by retrieving his brother's fortune from the Intendant's villainous hands, but also the urgency behind his desire since he only has 'a month or two of life to do it in'. To achieve good is admirable, and yet there is a hint of personal gain in the earnestness of his imperative: 'Must punish you, Maffeo. I cannot afford to cast away a chance.' Also, his air of humility is conveyed perhaps too frequently (four times within twenty lines), so that it becomes tinged with the suggestion of a conveniently assumed pose. It is perhaps too easy to give up a 'preferred' poverty in order to protect 'the poor and ignorant' from being seduced by the Intendant's 'pomp'; it seems complacent to admit his own trespass while arguing that he will not compound his sin by allowing others to trespass (which is just a

sophisticated version of the platitude 'do as I say, not as I do'); and
when the Pope 'enjoins' him to take 'all pains' to recover his
brother's estate 'as guardian of the infant's heritage for the Church',
the fine liturgical flourish should not obscure the simple fact that the
Church wants the land and the Bishop means to get it. His plans,
however, depend on Pippa's being dead so that he can punish her
murderer, the Intendant; consequently when Maffeo, the
Intendant, informs him to the contrary, his composure is suddenly
shaken. After long speeches of controlled and fluent rhetoric the
Bishop shows his first real emotion as he retorts swiftly and angrily:
'Liar!'. The single word, an artful stroke by Browning,[11] reveals the
Monsignor's immediate annoyance that his plans might be thwarted and his disbelief that his information could be wrong. He now
loses the initiative in the situation and says nothing, except to deny
again the Intendant's claim: 'I see through the trick, caitiff! I would
you spoke truth for once.' Even after Pippa's song he is only
marginally articulate. Making no direct comment on the lyric, he
springs up at the line 'Suddenly God took me', which is a reminder
of the short time he has to live, but there is still nothing to indicate
that he believes Maffeo's story about Pippa. Indeed, everything he
says before the song shows his reluctance to believe it,[12] and his
command to 'Gag this villain' after the song suggests an impulse to
silence Maffeo before he hears any more. The Monsignor's response
to Pippa thus reveals the depth of his desire to obey the Church's
order and confiscate the estate while the chance remains, but the
rest is uncertain. When the Bishop says of Maffeo 'He dares . . . I
know not half he dares', he demonstrates his indecision about
Maffeo's story, and though Pippa precipitates the final action, the
blunted coherence of his speech makes his intentions far from
defined. The Monsignor's selfhood has rested upon a deeply felt
identification with the Church, which has enabled him to assume
that God was always his confederate and to foster an image of
benevolent Christian humility; now, when threatened with the
possibility of not being able to fulfil the Church's task before he dies,
his strongest impulses are simply to conclude the business by
apprehending the Intendant.[13]

In each scene Pippa's influence has been marginal. Rather than
attaining any new moral insight or making any enlightened moral
judgement, her listeners show how they adapt the world to their
private purposes, demonstrating an innate self-centredness in their
pursuit of an ideal. The irony is that they achieve self-definition on
the basis of a self-conceived illusion, and it is. an irony which

Browning will continue to dramatise in his monologues, where the
reader is able to observe even more clearly characters who are 'self-
conceived, self-defined, and self-deceived'.[14]

If Pippa's songs have less effect on lives than might be thought,
what of Pippa herself? Her initial delight in the new dawn is marked
by her appropriation of the day as her own (Intr.19): the 'long blue
solemn hours' and 'fitful sunshine-minutes' shall all be hers
(Intr.25). It is a natural attitude on her part with which it is easy to
sympathise, since this is her holiday, her one chance to gather
'sufficient strength' for the following year's toil in the mill; yet her
possessiveness, emphasised by Browning's changes for 1849, reveals
a nascent, if innocuous, selfishness even in the paragon.[15] Pippa,
though not without knowledge, is unformed. She desires not just
happiness, but sufficient importance to impress her personality on
things, to exert some influence on people:

> Now, one thing I should like to really know:
> How near I ever might approach all these
> I only fancied being, this long day:
> – Approach, I mean, so as to touch them, so
> As to . . . in some way . . . move them – if you please,
> Do good or evil to them some slight way.
> . . . Ah me, and my important part with them,
> This morning's hymn half promised when I rose!
>
> (IV.ii.99–109)

Her indifference about the outcome ('good or evil') shows it is *her*
effectiveness that matters. Earlier in the play she exercises her
limited authority by flaunting her dominion over the flowers ('I am
queen of thee, floweret!'), commanding them to worship her
(Intr.95–103), and the inference may be that if she *were* to inherit
the mills, she would become like everybody else in their self-bound
assertiveness.

Illusion plays an obviously prominent role in Pippa's experience.
She embarks on a romantic quest for love and adventure, engaging
in a series of encounters which will furnish her with happiness and
strength for future labour. But her quest is a fiction; she does not
meet the real world, apart from the local prostitutes briefly; it is for
her a failed quest, vicarious from the outset and inevitably
unfulfilled. The pattern of Pippa's emotional stress, from a sun-
suffused dawn to the 'drear dark close' of her day, resembles a
similar transition in several of Keats's poems: from the allurement of

a dream to the waking on 'the cold hill's side', from the ecstasy of a
'light-winged Dryad' to the melancholy return to the 'sole self'. For
Keats such a pattern recognises the imagination's inability to
sustain the illusion and the unfailing incursion of the physical world.
The poet of negative capability may lose all sense of self through
absorption in other things, but such experience is transitory, subject
to vicissitude and time. Pippa seeks release from hardship through a
similar act of negative capability – by becoming someone else she
may share their happiness – but time for her too 'passes' and
Browning, as well as Keats, recognises the intrusions of a severe
reality. These elements of negative capability have been emphasised by David Shaw in order to argue that the play is about Pippa's
powers of 'sympathetic imagination',[16] yet this view seems to me not
to account for either Pippa's motivations or the change in her
feelings. For example, the self-indulgent basis of her imaginative
play is shown in the way she assumes the identity of Asolan citizens
'in order to receive love, not to return it'.[17] Professor Shaw says
Pippa 'wants to flow over into other people', whereas she wishes
more to appropriate their happiness, approaching them with
superiority and being able to reject their situation if the matter were
not a fancy:

> – Not envy, sure! – for if you gave me
> Leave to take or to refuse,
> In earnest, do you think I'd choose
> That sort of new love to enslave me?   (Intr.157–60)

Nor does she want 'to savor the bride's "snow-pure cheek" and
"black bright tresses"'.[18] She actually disdains Phene's attractiveness as being too fragile to touch: 'are not such / Used to be tended,
flowerlike, every feature, / As if one's breath would fray the lily of a
creature?' (Intr.143–5). Browning shows the limitations rather than
the achievements of negative capability, since for him the reality
which invades imaginative experience includes the perceiving self,
which may distort sympathetic identification:

> The bee with his comb,
> The mouse at her dray,
> The grub in his tomb,
> Wile winter away;
> But the fire-fly and hedge-shrew and lob-worm, I pray,
> How fare they?   (iv.ii.1–6)

Here, for example, the first four lines evoke the protective domesticity of small creatures, though clouded slightly by the implicit threat in 'tomb', and to this point Pippa is absorbed in their nature. In the last two lines, however, her conscious mind asserts itself to question the security of natural order. The lines echo her first song which accepted the operation of things as in accord with God's presence, but here Pippa is suddenly unsure about any providential plan for infinitesimal and ephemeral beings and her negative capability is no longer sustained. The source of Browning's success in the play lies rather in the ironies of the egotistical sublime than in negative capability. If Pippa as a singer of songs is to symbolise poetic creation, then Browning is well aware of the interfering ego in both artist and audience.[19]

Any irony reflecting on Pippa's ego does not, however, prevent the reader from responding sympathetically to her ebullient spirits in the Introduction and to her reflective pathos in the Conclusion. Through her the reader is able to participate in the search for some illusory satisfaction, for the comfort of reciprocated love, and so in the context of Pippa's situation – her one day's respite and her desire for importance – her return to the hymn in the last lines becomes evidence of a longing for religious solace.[20] The final irony for the reader is that Pippa's hymn may function for her as her songs do for others, as some external reinforcement of the personality's innate desire, and in this sense Pippa too has made God her confederate. There is no reason to think that Pippa herself views the hymn with any significant religious feeling; she simply accepts it with a mixture of nonchalance and disappointed hope as containing truth 'some way or other'.

This attitude, twice repeated by her, that the hymn is 'True in some sense or other', should also provide a clue to ironies surrounding the hymn's theme about all men being God's puppets. Everyone is either a puppet or trying to be a puppet-master in 'some way'. Sebald has been a 'slave' to Ottima, who attempts in the first episode to regain her control; the students are exploiting Phene in order to trick Jules; Jules eventually uses Phene himself; Luigi is manipulated by political schemers; Bluphocks is paid by the Intendant; the poor girls are the servants of whoever can pay for the privilege; the Monsignor attempts to control the Intendant and is himself ruled by the Church; and Pippa's very survival has been engineered by Maffeo. More pertinently, each, whatever his degree of freedom, is the victim of his illusions and the puppet of his own desires. Sebald becomes the slave of his outraged morality, or a slave to his sense of being a slave; Jules is the puppet of his aesthetic idealism; Luigi is impelled by his desire for heroic action; and the Monsignor is motivated by his wish to obey the Church before he dies. The protagonists, as suggested, are not led to any new moral awareness, and so the ironic ambiguities in the climactic action of each episode illustrate their false belief in their freedom of choice. Nor can Pippa directly choose her own destiny, which explains why the final episode is about her possible inheritance: she is a pawn in the Intendant's schemes so that even the innocent cannot escape the web of human intrigue. The notion that all are God's puppets is ironic, for they seem rather the puppets of their idealistic view of themselves, and Pippa's lyrics serve to remind them of their illusions, strengthening the net of individual consciousness. At the same time, this does not mean that Browning has written a dramatically negative satire. To observe that selfhood is pursued in terms of a preconceived illusion and therefore subject to moral deception is to observe an irony which may exist potentially in any search for individual identity, but it is not necessarily to scorn the whole process of self-definition. Browning's emphasis on the psychology of each action, leaving the morality, even sometimes the action itself obscured, means that he stresses the humanity of his characters. Each protagonist does *act* in terms of his ideals, which are thus an index to personality, a means of *identifying* the self, as well as a prison of illusion, a means of *justifying* the self. We do sense that this assertion of personality is therefore a positive result in each episode, despite the dubious morality. Whatever the weakness of the justification, or of the idealism, it nevertheless produces some sense of identity, some centre of being which holds the personality together. This relationship between identity and justification also shows the link between belief in self and belief in God's approval, how deception about the former is transformed into an illusion of the latter. Yet, Browning does not leave any easy conclusion. If the reader wishes to argue further that by being puppets of their own desires these characters are in fact being God's puppets, enacting His purposes by being themselves, the concluding irony remains that free will is an illusion, with God, as I suggested earlier, the ironist.

The use of irony in literature usually supplies a satisfactory intellectual perspective for the reader, whose enjoyment is increased by the necessary detachment which results from recognising it. However, the detachment is balanced here by sympathy for Pippa, so that the reader's intellectual superiority over the mesh of illusions is matched by his emotional awareness of the human need for that illusion. Pippa herself can give no acceptable intellectual or moral appraisal of life in Asolo: that she returns from the mélange of duplicity and vanity without corruption is hardly a triumph when it is remembered that her encounters with the society are illusory. She has 'passed' reality, not met it. Nevertheless, the attractiveness of her quiet acquiescence in the sad recognition that all was finally a 'game' remains a force in the play, allowing the reader to experience her comparatively uncorrupted view of the world and her need for some, even fictive, consolation. At the same time, the reader is expected to sustain this view without relinquishing his detachment from it. Browning's irony therefore provides us with the dual vision of melancholy innocence and knowing scepticism, of the necessity for illusion and the awareness of its limitations. In this way Phene's realistic appraisal of the way men appropriate God is balanced by Pippa's consolatory thoughts about the way God appropriates men.

The psychology of self-centred idealism with its implied solitariness is reinforced structurally by the juxtaposition of disparate scenes. The drama is episodic because the points of view are subjective private worlds of different mood and quality, but into this kaleidoscopic fragmentation Browning thrusts an obvious patterning based on the recurrence of Pippa's intrusions. The problem of regarding Pippa as the unifying focus in the play is that her view is dispersed as the work proceeds, and despite the Introduction, the youthful lyricism of each song comes as an emotional shock in the midst of the highly wrought intensities of each scene. However, each shock effects spreading ripples of irony, and unity ultimately depends more on irony than on the character of Pippa. While introducing an element of contrivance, the repetitive device of the songs achieves its success through the resulting ironies, though it does place the onus of balancing its facets on the reader.[21] In drawing attention to itself through its use of excessive coincidence, the design makes the work both a totality and an obvious artifice: as totality, the design embraces the ironies in private illusion and social intrigue, and as artifice it sustains the reader's detachment, reminding him of his own participation as observer of the irony. As totality, the design shows the apparent coincidence between the author's plan and God's plan, but as artifice it reminds the reader that any plan is after all only a fiction.

Much of this may seem a distinctively modern reading of the

drama. However, though such issues are usually a matter of degree, there seems little question that Browning was one of the first to develop the poetry of impersonality which is a feature of twentieth-century verse, relying as it does far more on the audience than did previous poetry of overheard lyricism, and it is tempting to observe several other aspects of *Pippa Passes* which anticipate modern attitudes. For example, Pippa's cyclical return to the starting point of her quest implies what Northrop Frye has called, in connection with Nietzsche's Zarathustra, 'a cosmology of identical recurrence',[22] a cosmology which is both appalling because of its endless futility and comforting because of its predictable security. The recurring coincidence of Pippa's intrusions and the placing of her one day's holiday between two years of repetitive toil intensify the same idea. But the important point is that *Pippa Passes* is in itself a deft literary experiment once its tragicomic elements are realised. The characters are caught in attitudes and personalities which deny them freedom while they think they exercise it – to *them* Pippa's songs lead them to a free choice. Yet the illusion of choice is essential to their personal security. In my view it is the portrayal of the ironies attached to imprisonment within subjectivity, combined with the need for assuring reinforcement of that subjectivity, which makes this one of Browning's first mature works, even though it is something of a transition piece between his stage plays and the monologues. Any sense of a diffuse focus is redeemed by the subtlety of mixed perspectives, and the whole is distinguished by an irony which leaves the reader both aloof and with a chastened sense of human frailty that may even include (my God!) himself.

3 The Drama of Self-Conception

All speech is an act: all expression potentially a pose. Such is the truism on which drama is founded. As Fra Celestino warns in *The Ring and the Book*,

> who trusts
> To human testimony for a fact
> Gets this sole fact–himself is proved a fool;
> Man's speech being false.

Browning seems to have realised quite early the implications for character of this falsity in 'human testimony', and his use of the hidden artifices in language and of the ironies they produce leads him away from the more Romantic forms of lyrical self-expression, as found in Keats and Shelley, to more modern forms of dramatic poetry. A concern with linguistic contrivance constantly underlies his focus on argument and there is therefore the sense that contrivance is fundamental to his portrayal of character. His more admirable characters as well as the less desirable ones manipulate language or describe themselves in terms of figurative conceits, so that it is not enough to note that Browning reveals people using language deceitfully. He goes deeper, to portray through a fusion of poetry and psychology their struggle with images of self-conception, and in that drama, however unwittingly, self-dramatisation is a constant ploy.

Normally in speech the manipulative aspects are overlooked or perhaps suppressed in the interests of articulating meaning. It is when attention is drawn to the use of language that its histrionic elements become apparent, and this is particularly likely to occur when the aims of self-expression, the communication of feeling and

thought, are extended into the aims of self-definition or the fixing
and description of identity. The usually unconscious or at least
unstated effort to realise self-understanding in addition to self-
expression is what so often leads monologuists into dramatising
themselves. There are a variety of ways in which this act may occur,
but as would be expected in a literary art form it is generally a
matter of linguistic contrivance, an image or metaphor or perhaps
some broader strategy, a pose or proposition taken up in the course
of the argument. It is obvious, of course, that in a monologue all we
have are the inflexions and patterns of a single voice, and that
consequently the artifices of language reflect the qualities of the
speaker, the character whom the author simulates. What seems less
obvious is that it is the function of language, the psychological
purpose of its use, rather than what is said or meant, which is often
most character-revealing. What the reader is drawn into, then, is an
apprehension of the function as well as the meaning of language,
where he may be required to distinguish between the use of
language for expressive purposes and its use for other more
ambiguous purposes. It is in the shifts between these two functions,
the expressive and the dramatic, or in the act of combining both,
that the drama of self-consciousness takes place.

Consider, for example, the opening line of 'Soliloquy of the
Spanish Cloister': 'Gr-r-r–there go, my heart's abhorrence!'
While at first glance this seems simply an expression of anger and
hatred, on closer inspection a contrast emerges between the
inarticulate utterance of the growl and the polysyllabic diction of
'heart's abhorrence'. To describe an object of hate as in this phrase is
to formalise the feeling into an acceptable Latinate abstraction, and
such an act represents a split in the speaker's consciousness between
impulsive feeling and shaped perception. In this instance it is a
schism basic to his self-deception and comic in its incongruity, and a
similar disjunction between emotion and expression operates
throughout the poem to indicate the way bitter, destructive
frustrations underlie a surface pose, an arrangement of what the
speaker conceives to be a pious self. Browning generates the conflict
in the opening line and it is a function of the speaker's utterance, of
the fusion of dramatisation and expression as he formulates his
feelings and perceptions, allowing one to inform the other.

Browning's poetry illustrates a variety of histrionic acts, from this
less obtrusive example to more overt forms of self-dramatisation,
such as that in 'Rudel to the Lady of Tripoli', where Rudel quite

deliberately selects the sunflower as an emblem of his sacrificial love. The consciousness of his choice allows Rudel to combine self-knowledge – he is aware that the sunflower is 'but a foolish mimic sun' – with the earnestness of his devotion; the metaphor is both self-expressive, in that his concern is solely for the 'East' like the sunflower's concern which is 'solely for the sun', and a self-dramatisation, in that the image displays himself as an offering, 'outspread like a sacrifice / Before its idol'. In this instance Rudel is committed to his emblem and conscious of its implications, but characters are not always so conscious of their impulses. At the end of Guido's second monologue in *The Ring and the Book*, Guido's defences are finally stripped away and he is left as an undefined emotional energy, striving feverishly to survive. Judged guilty of murdering Pompilia and her foster-parents, he faces the guillotine with no further prospect of saving his life through the dramatic devices which had earlier marked his trial speech. Yet in this last scramble for help there is still the effect of the histrionic:

> I am the Granduke's – no, I am the Pope's!
> Abate, – Cardinal, – Christ, – Maria, – God. . . .
> Pompilia, will you let them murder me?

In clinging to a sense of vindication in his use of the word 'murder', Guido projects himself as a victim, a wronged man about to be destroyed by authority and deserving the pity even of those whom he hated and himself murdered. Here Browning seems to indicate that even in failure and despair there is the vain impulse to dramatise.

II

A familiar example of a character who projects an image is the Duke of Ferrara in 'My Last Duchess' and several critics have observed that the Duke stages a show for the envoy.[1] Through what appear to be admissions of uncertainty, he conveys the air of a man revealing his past with frankness and spontaneity:

> She had
> A heart – how shall I say?   (ll. 21–2)

> She thanked men, – good! but thanked
> Somehow – I know not how –   (ll. 31–2)

But he knows very well how:

> as if she ranked
> My gift of a nine-hundred-years-old name
> With anybody's gift.   (ll. 32–4)

These parenthetical phrases are clearly devices to manipulate the envoy, and the Duke is deliberate rather than spontaneous.[2] For instance, his apparently magnanimous gesture of taking the envoy beside him – 'Nay, we'll go / Together down, Sir!' – serves only to dramatise his authority further, based as it is on the Duke's power to make the gesture at all. He must, as we all know, maintain scrupulous control over his life and surroundings; when the vitality of the first Duchess disturbs his equanimity, she is transformed into an art-object which he can then control, pulling the curtain to reveal her smile when *he* chooses. A jealous director who cannot tolerate action which he does not determine, he must always portray himself as a man who is in absolute charge of his life, redeeming the past and transforming it into a present where his aristocratically defined identity is no longer threatened, and the climactic dramatis-ation of this selfhood lies in the cause-and-effect relationship between his giving of 'commands' and 'all smiles' stopping 'together'. The result is an aesthetic effect which satisfies his sense of form: the Duchess now stands there 'As if alive'. His constant concern with artefacts, ordering an illusion to replace actuality, is a means of eradicating the contingency of life while retaining its beauty and shape, but the loss of the Duchess' spontaneity is a clue to the loss of vitality which accompanies this process, both for the Duke's art and for his personality: the art which surrounds him reflects the artifice of his character.

His skill with language, combined with the authority of his social position, mean he is able to act out here an unchallenged performance which both creates and reinforces an ideal of the ego as monarch of all. So powerful is the illusion that he even assigns his own thoughts to other people:

> never read
> Strangers like you that pictured countenance,
> The depth and passion of its earnest glance,
> But to myself they turned (since none puts by

The curtain I have drawn for you, but I)
And seemed as they would ask me, if they durst,
How such a glance came there; so, not the first
Are you to turn and ask thus.   (ll. 6–13)

But the envoy has not asked 'thus' and nor has anyone else, since that is only what they 'would' have asked if they dared. Their enquiring gesture, turning to him, could mean several things. The specific question about the glance is therefore the Duke's own supposition and part of his presumption that people think what he imposes on them. Thus he recovers his social persona through an act of self-dramatising which absorbs other people's actions into his own explanatory narrative. Since they dare not intrude upon it, the fiction is preserved. What his visitors say afterwards is irrelevant, as long as it does not enter his consciousness and as long as they continue to play the supporting role which sustains his authority. The Duke's obvious success in his performance means he more easily identifies with his part; while the repetition of pulling the curtain before strangers suggests the continuing need to remake and reinforce the desired persona, his conscious mind acknowledges no other self, in himself or in others, and so he *is* the constructed persona, his own mask. This identification does not occur without cost, however, for the monarchy of the ego requires a domination of self as well as others, and the control over his own artifice means the loss of his own spontaneity of response – an irony which underlies his pretended frankness. He must suppress all feeling and compassion since they, like the Duchess, may be disruptive, perhaps even suggesting the value in other points of view, and just as he turns her into an artefact so he makes his own personality into an impressively controlled form, precisely and masterfully sustained, as if alive. It is a destructive identity because whatever does not conform to its demands is excised. The Duke's shaping of self and world therefore reveals a formidable solipsism, the process and consequences of a belief in self which is supported by a rationalised disbelief in the value of any other perspective.

Another early monologue which portrays a different means of asserting self-importance is 'Johannes Agricola in Meditation'. Instead of the Duke's obsession with secular control, Agricola seeks the more permanent advantage of spiritual power. As he claims to look each night 'right through' heaven's 'gorgeous roof', he immediately asserts a visionary capacity beyond other mortals and

quickly demonstrates the strength of his desire to associate himself
with the highest authority:

> For I intend to get to God,
>   For 't is to God I speed so fast.   (ll. 6–7)

What begins as a goal is then transformed into a predestined
actuality, through shifting the mood of the verb from a subjunctive
which implies a future culmination when he will 'lay' his spirit down
in God's breast 'at last', to a present indicative where all is
accomplished: 'I lie where I have always lain' (l. 11). He represents
himself as God's child, predetermined as such before the heavens
were made, and he basks in God's love: 'thought and word and
deed/All go to swell his love for me,/Me . . .' (ll. 26–8). The
repetition of the personal pronoun emphasises the importance of
this realisation of self as an object of God's love, but not satisfied
with this he claims that he is even necessary to God's love, not just its
object but its 'content'. He was made, he says,

>   because that love had need
> Of something irreversibly
> Pledged solely its content to be.   (ll.28–30)

The potency of this role allows him to exploit again a mixing of
tenses, this time conflating past, present and future into the present
tense illusion of gazing down from heaven on those in hell,
'Swarming in ghastly wretchedness' (l. 45). The temporal confusion
reinforces naturally the concept of predestination with its denial of
everyday sequential experience. The order of events does not matter
and this interruption of the normal process of causality, achieved
here through manipulating the syntax of time, provides Agricola
with considerable power: he may drink poison with impunity, for
instance. Yet despite the inflated self-importance which his identity
as chosen favourite conveys, he does 'pledge' himself to God; his
manner is generally quiet and he concludes in humility:

> God, whom I praise; how could I praise,
>   If such as I might understand,
> Make out and reckon on his ways,
>   And bargain for his love. . . ?   (ll. 56–9)

In a sense he conforms to the Christian paradox of self-abnegation – he submits the self to God's love and defines his identity accordingly. But in effect it is only the parody of submission. Apart from the ironic contradiction that in the face of his explanation of God's 'need' (l. 28) it is finally his inability to explain God which reinforces his belief, his exaggeration of the effects of that belief and the exclusiveness which he claims for the results show that he is concerned with self-definition rather than self-denial. Agricola feigns selflessness in order to aggrandise the self, projecting this pose as a fiction of identity, a necessary requirement of his desire for salvation.

The contrivances of language are largely suggested in these two poems by elements of tone and manner of speech, in the way the Duke represents his actions or Agricola represents his relationship with God. Sometimes, however, the artifice of the dramatisation is indicated by emotional expressions which reveal a different level of responsiveness, such as occur in 'Pictor Ignotus'. The speaker in this poem, the unknown painter, is caught in the act of defending his adherence to conventional styles of art. He could paint, if he wished, in the new manner which is so praised, he claims, and he has indeed been tempted by fame, but he chose to reject popular acclaim and instead devoted himself to religious work. The torment lies in his awareness of the implications of that choice. He admits that his heart sinks with the monotony of painting 'the same series, Virgin, Babe and Saint', but comforts himself with the thought that he at least avoids the fickleness of 'vain tongues' and the trafficking of merchants. The point of the monologue, then, is to assuage his own doubt, and he attempts to portray himself as a man who has faced the alternatives and chosen wisely. But the mask of confidence is precariously realised. His apparent self-awareness in facing both the desire for fame and the death of his mouldering paintings comes increasingly to suggest a necessary self-protection which avoids implications about his own lack of fulfilment.

The poem is based on the shape of his underlying argument: 'I could have painted. . . . But a voice changed it. . . . Wherefore I chose my portion'. This is the structure of his rationalised confidence. Partly a narrative of past desires and dreams, partly an act of persuasion, it is the justification which he requires in order to overcome his threatening despair. The recognition that nothing prevented him from painting in the new manner, no 'bar', no 'fate', makes the justification even more necessary, since the responsibility is entirely his – a 'thought which saddens while it soothes!' (l. 3). If the choice was his own, so were the consequences, and so too was the cause, in the 'voice' which changed his dreams. The voice is his reaction to the dream of fame, largely a fear of public judgement, and the interruptions and broken statements in the passage (ll. 41–9) imply the spontaneity of an honest moment.[3] But the degree of awareness which the painter has of his fear is unclear and his similes suggest that dramatisation occurs even here in obviously emotional responses. Glimpses of the sights of fame in his dreams have scared him, 'like the revels through a door / Of some strange house of idols at its rites!' Two lines later, he asks,

> Who summoned those cold faces that begun
> To press on me and judge me? Though I stooped
>   Shrinking, as from the soldiery a nun,
> They drew me forth, and spite of me . . . enough!   (ll. 46–9)

Both these images represent his dread of the unknown and suggest the depth of his insecurities about the external world away from the protection of convention and cloister. The rape particularly indicates this: he seems afraid of some violent destruction at the hands of the world. But each image also shows how he unconsciously chooses to reinforce his fears by justifying them: the first image of 'revels' represents his desires as some illicit, sacrilegious indulgence deserving to be shunned, and to see himself as a nun shrinking from soldiers is clearly a sympathetic piece of self-representation. Although he acknowledges these emotions by expressing them, he is saved from examining their validity by the way he expresses them. His anxiety about exposure and personal attack is brushed aside ('enough!') rather than accommodated, and he concentrates instead on the more obvious threat of public pettiness. Near the end of the poem there is another emotional cry which registers his dismay as he realises his failure: 'So, die my pictures! surely, gently die!' (l. 69). There is a sense of reconciliation to the inevitable, but also an element of self-dramatisation again, contained in the pathos of the adverbs 'surely, gently'. In this outburst the painter laments his own loss, projecting himself as a tragic figure, worthy of self-pity. In a final series of rhetorical questions he addresses the youth whose paintings are now highly praised. The rhetoric should affirm that contact with the world contaminates purity, but the questioning still seems to suggest an uncertainty about the answer, that the rhetorical affirmation is a verbal pose. These elements of the histrionic reveal the internal struggles of a man who cannot develop his potential because he does not face the realities of his own desires and fears; instead of braving his insecurities, he reinforces them through an identity which justifies them. In fearing the unknown he has ironically predetermined that he become the unknown.

It should be clear, I think, that in Browning's poetry self-dramatisation is not merely the obvious use of imagery to portray mood or states of mind; it is linked with basic elements of personality, and in some poems may be combined with consciousness of the process to provide an even more complex drama of conflicting needs and shifting realisations about the self. 'James Lee's Wife', in *Dramatis Personae*, is an example. There are nine sections in this poem which represent the changing perceptions of a woman who is in difficulties about love. Again, the images which she uses show her projection of herself: in section II she expresses sympathy for sailors taking their chance on the ocean, but this sympathy emerges from the sense of her own impending wreck on the voyage of love and indicates her view of herself as a sailor who needs God's help. As well as this dramatisation there are also intrusive bursts of feeling – in phrases such as 'would I knew!' or 'now, gnash your teeth!' – which release the conflicting surges of a desire for help and pity and a bitter awareness of the growing hopelessness in the situation. The wife works by analogy in almost every section and she reveals in the process both the self-image which she projects as her action within each mood and her relationship to that image, though the latter varies from direct expression of feeling to the perplexed attempt to understand what is happening (as in section III: 'why must cold spread?'). The result is a fluctuating tone and a severe sense of conflict between the need to understand and direct emotional reaction. Indeed, one of the elements in the drama is her struggle to attain composure: 'I will be quiet and talk with you', she says to her husband (section IV).

She also demonstrates a growing capacity for irony, at the expense of the young poet in section VI, for instance, as she exposes his assumption of superiority: 'His triumph, in eternity/Too plainly manifest!'. Towards the end of the same section she shifts between a vain effort to rejoice in mutability ('Rise with it, then!') and a bitter

awareness of the irony for man that 'all he'd sink to save' is washed
away by time. In this she is able both to express the 'sting' of change
and to detach herself from it through being conscious of its ironies.
Later, in section IX, she mixes an even larger number of tones,
dramatising herself as the worthless, graceless object which, she
implies, is how her husband must see her, acknowledging the
gesture ('Conceded!'), seeking in turn an admission from him that if
he would unlock his soul with the key of love he might see her as she
sees him, detaching herself from the request ('strange plea'), though
unable to resist its point (that it would not matter then if she were
the 'ill-favoured one'), and going on to evoke a reverie about the
future, a hypothesis, built on subjunctives ('How strange it
were . . .'), that should he be touched with one element of love like
hers, he might become like her, grow coarse and gnarled, but she
would then neither know nor care once she was 'dead of joy'. The
whole section is a classic combination of threat, play for sympathy,
recrimination and claims of loyalty as she constantly urges her own
total and consistent devotion. It also demonstrates the construction
of an increased complexity of consciousness, as she asserts
possibilities, listens to her own reaction and defends her feelings, and
the drama of the poem lies in the reflexiveness of shifts and thrusts of
phrasing as she struggles to register and understand her own
changing reality. In the beginning when faced with images of
change, her reaction is to portray herself as part of a series of
necessary relationships:

> Thou art a man,
>   But I am thy love.
> For the lake, its swan;
>   For the dell, its dove.

When 'At the Window' (section I) she cannot dissociate herself from
the conventions of companionship, but in the last stanzas of section
VI she demonstrates a more complex psychological action as she
moves to an emotional identification with the wind's moaning
expression of universal vicissitude, while maintaining an intellectual observation about enduring God's 'act' and being unable to
substantiate anything. At the same time this effort to accommodate
uncertainty and flux is surrounded by episodes which reinforce her
original ideas: her analogy of the butterfly in section V reflects her
belief about the transforming powers of love, and her metaphor of

the earth in section VII affirms her belief in earthly duty with a heavenly reward. Consequently, the separation between sections highlights the threat in her situation of an identity fragmented into conflicting selves, and her growing self-awareness becomes an act of psychological necessity, an effort to cope with the conflicts of self-doubt and self-assertion. Her husband's changed feelings have forced her to question her identity as 'wife', yet she finds it hard to relinquish the original role. In the end she makes a final attempt to sustain her identity and continuity with the past through the fiction of a hypothetical future, which if achieved (if he became her) would serve as an ironic vindication of her original self-conception.

In 'The Worst of It', another from the *Dramatis Personae* volume, the situation of 'James Lee's Wife' is reversed and it is the husband who responds to an unfaithful wife. On the surface this poem is perhaps less engaging than others since it depends more on fluctuations and abruptness, more on the sparseness and looseness of direct speech than on images or rhetoric; yet it portrays the fine poise of an ambivalent judgement which is conveyed through the possibilities of a histrionic self. The drama lies less in the antagonism between speaker and auditor than in how much the speaker believes what he says,[4] in his uncertainty as he attempts to shape a role for himself in this new situation. The first part of the poem is governed by his melodramatic relationship of the swan and the beast. He dramatises himself as the worthless partner, but his expression develops into the excessiveness of parody which makes the image a fiction he cannot really believe in. By the third stanza the admission that he was 'the speckled beast' who taught his wife 'to stoop' begins to ring hollow through sheer repetitiveness of tone and idea, so that what begins as self-abasement ('I that am nothing') becomes transformed into a parody of *her* view of him, of the superior attitude which allowed her to break her vows. Yet he cannot dismiss her so easily, being essentially trapped by the image of her angel-like beauty, and his idealising of her features into aesthetic abstractions – 'the brow / That looked like marble and smelt like myrrh' (ll. 38–9) – means, through its self-determining evidence of her value, that he cannot accept her total ruination in punishment: 'Hardly! That must be understood!' (l. 43). Therefore he is equivocal, unsure about what he thinks: 'What shall I say or do?' (l. 97). Images are no longer to be trusted, so he now rejects what men tell him is beauty and truth as mere falsehood and mask (ll. 85–6), and he eventually structures his ambivalence as an antithesis between frozen affection and inflamed thoughts: 'my heart feels ice while my words breathe flame' (l. 108).

These images suggest both the awareness of rationalised complexities or impassioned argument and the emotional numbness where he was once full of desire, and this sense of an antithetical confusion between feeling and conception is central to the poem's psychological conflict. The dramatic relationship between the speaker and his wife which he develops in the opening stanzas conforms to his perception of his wife's value, but that value proposes a role for himself which he is now unable to identify with, and consequently the images of beast and swan become increasingly ironic. The changing tone registers a growing detachment from his own expressions which is in effect a crisis of self-conception, and this crisis becomes focused mainly on his role as judge. Through imagining himself 'called at last / When the devil stabs you, to lend the knife' (ll. 53–4), he objectifies his desire for justice, but he is caught between a generosity of concern which seeks justice for his wife and an instinctive sense of injury which seeks justice for himself. In private he is bothered by his conscience (ll. 80–2) and in his dreams he regrets the way she is treated, 'my swan's obtaining the crow's rebuff' (l. 84), but the need to protect his sense of personal righteousness is too strong and he cannot bring himself to make any public acknowledgement of her. His final dramatisation is therefore of his ultimate role in heaven, where he will maintain a pose of injured gentility, publicly ignoring her:

> I knew you once: but in Paradise,
>   If we meet, I will pass nor turn my face.   (ll. 113–14)

It is a role which reflects his own needs rather than his wife's, and this outward denial hides inner misgivings. Such a proposed identity even hints that his wishes for her happiness may be a fiction, not genuinely meant since merely part of a self-dramatisation which makes him in his own eyes seem generous and thereby vindicating his decision. The 'worst of it' may be several things to him – his uncertain judgement and conflicting feelings, that she fell because of him, or that she may be glad she deceived him – but I suspect the worst of it is really the possibility that she may have been right to leave him, that indeed she may 'Have done no evil and want no aid' (l. 101). Understandably, that is a possibility which he can only dramatise with ironic ambiguity.

III

The poems so far have provided examples of characters engaged in varying forms of self-definition. In each a linguistic act is generated in order to meet some need for self-understanding which is implicit in the situation, and the dramatisation is essentially an attempt at self-discovery, to affirm identity or gain some perspective on it. The Duke of Ferrara, Johannes Agricola, and the unknown painter all act within a world shaped by their own selection of images, and when the wife of James Lee and the speaker in 'The Worst of It' find their identities as lover are questioned, dramatisation becomes a means of exploring their situation, discovering or perhaps avoiding its possibilities.[5] Dramatic intensity is thus gained through each character's immersion in a relationship, sometimes unconscious, with his fictionalised self. However, the means of self-generation are clearly various and while there are not exclusive categories – poems often combine several methods – I should outline some of the possibilities.

One direct, if not always obvious, method of self-projection is through narrative. A character may narrate events in order to control his role in them, as in 'Porphyria's Lover', to discover some reality amidst subjective transferences, as in 'Childe Roland to the Dark Tower Came', or to regret the loss of some potential identity in a wasted opportunity from the past, perhaps in relation to present dissatisfaction, as in 'Youth and Art'. In 'The Confessional' the distraught speaker tells what happened as an expression of her terrible frustration and outrage at the deception played upon her, but the narrative also effectively portrays herself as a victim of clerical deceit, which understandably avoids the horrific aspect of her role as unwitting accomplice. Both 'Count Gismond' and 'Saul', poems quite different in tone, also recount past events, in the first instance in order to relive an identity as the heroine gallantly rescued from disgrace, and in the second as a means of understanding a strange mystical event – David's re-creation of his experience with Saul is a retelling which objectifies his role as visionary poet.

Sometimes the temporal ordering of narrative may figure more prominently, not so much to define a character in relationship to a sequence of events, as to elaborate the way temporal awareness may influence self-conception. Such a concern ranges from the Bishop of St Praxad's, who remains absorbed in his triumphs when he won the mistress, and Fra Lippo Lippi, who bases his present paradox as a spiritual monk with physical vitality on his boyhood poverty when bread was a more powerful incentive than self-knowledge, to the Duke of Ferrara, who uses his control over the past as a means of demonstrating his power over causation. To evoke images from memory is often, however, an ambiguous means of realising selfhood, since while it may lead to a freedom from past constraint through the release of defining images into a flux of changing awareness and shifting possibilities, such as occurs in 'Fra Lippo Lippi' or for Caponsacchi in *The Ring and the Book*, it may also lead to a trap of identification, as it is for the Bishop of St Praxad's or in the more complex web which evolves in 'By the Fireside'.

In 'By the Fireside' the speaker indulges in a curious reverie where he becomes detached from the present through projecting the recall of past events into a future activity – what he will do 'When the long dark autumn-evenings come'. He gives the impression of a consciousness which is fluid and expansive, and yet paradoxically it remains confined by the basically temporal structuring of his narrative. Time is fundamental, for temporal process is the evidence – 'see where the years conduct!' (st. xxvi) – that he is caught and defined by a temporal event, by the moment of union which is the focus for his memories: 'I am named and known by that moment's feat' (st. li). When he persuades his wife to join in the reverie he suggests a necessary deconstruction of the present:

> Let us now forget and now recall,
>   Break the rosary in a pearly rain,
> And gather what we let fall!   (st. xxx)

In this forgetting and breaking of the circle of security and devotion there is a potential creativity, the chance for reshaping the past and so for making a new self, but how much he alters the original event is not indicated and what he conveys is rather an impression of impotence in the face of superior forces. In the way his narrative is presented, he activates nothing, merely following the well-known hand wherever he is led (st. vi) and portraying himself through constructions of passive syntax as a passive victim moulded by outside action. During the November of their first meeting, when he fears to touch the 'last leaf', a solution is not found through his initiative, but through 'the best chance of all', when the leaf should 'unfasten itself' (st. xliii). The bar between the two people 'was broken' and they finally 'were mixed' – 'The forests had done it' (st. xlviii). The action of these forces is a little awesome in their contribution to the process of his making – 'How the world is made for each of us!' – just as the contingency of the event made it somewhat amazing: 'Oh, the little more and how much it is! / And the little less, and what worlds away!' (st. xxxix). Still, he cannot avoid the extraordinary success of the one moment of union which defined his existence. From it he took his 'station and degree' and his 'small life' grew 'complete' (st. li).

The poem is of course largely a reverie in tone, without the same persuasive aspects of a monologue; it is less an argument than a musing, a contemplation within an extended temporal context. Yet the lyric qualities of direct expressiveness are not allowed to stand; the speaker is too self-conscious for that and these exclamatory phrases contribute even further to a sense of the spectator-like stance of a monologuist. It is as if he is tacitly bemused by it all, detaching himself from the narrative through passive constructions which absolve him from responsibility and watching himself made, unable to play an active part in the process. There is a hint of rationalisation, then, as he relates his pattern of submission to some larger purpose, explaining the production of his soul's 'fruit' as a contribution to 'the general deed of man' (st. l), and the tone of mild wonderment returns again at the end when he expresses his intention of giving the whole matter more thought one day, 'When the autumn comes'.

I have stressed the sense of entrapment and this understated air of bemusement because they are elements of the play of consciousness in the poem which have received little attention, and because they lead to an even less obvious feature of the poem's function as a definition through narrative. While there is of course comfort and security in the speaker's marriage, a domestic calm in the fireside image, there is also the impression of a subtly insidious dissatisfaction, the suppressed realisation of a debilitating stasis. In the opening stanza, the speaker questions the whereabouts of his soul's 'pleasant hue', suggesting that like the soul's other voices it will be silent, 'dumb', in 'life's November too'. The adverb 'too' indicates the voices are silent now and while the tone of these lines is difficult to determine with any precision, they imply a lack of felicity, a sense that something is missing, or at least unexpressed, despite the security of knowing what he will do in the autumn evenings. Or is that the problem? In the heavy monosyllabic rhythm and repeated phrase of the way he will turn the page, and in the promise of prose instead of verse (st. ii) is the prospect of a monotonous, regulated existence. She is a 'perfect wife' (st. xxi), and 'nature obtained the best' of him (st. li), but how does perfection wear in time and if nature has had his best already, what is left now? He was born to love his wife (st. li), but also to watch her 'sink' back by the fireside (st. lii), and in twice describing how she sits 'mutely', there is perhaps a touch of weariness in the repeated phrase 'my heart knows how' (sts. xxiii, lii). Is it the comfort of a guaranteed responsiveness he feels (st. xxiv), or is it a weighty feeling, dull repetitiveness bearing the burden of a lifetime's meaning extended from the one ecstatic moment when they stepped outside themselves? When he seeks to affirm the belief that their life has led to 'an age so blest that by its side, / Youth seems the waste instead' (st. xxv), the concept is a question and is raised in the context of desiring reassurance: 'My own, confirm me!'. He also asks how 'the change' will strike them when they enter heaven, when they will understand 'The great Word which makes all things new' (st. xxvii), but the act of formulating the question seems clearly to suggest that he expects no change, that the transformations of death will bring no intrinsic alteration for those who have achieved spiritual union on earth. Indeed he even expresses his desire for such continuity, seeking his wife's guidance after death (st. xxviii), since a life defined by unity with another can only be sustained in eternity through continuing the identification, or so it seems to the speaker here. His reverie thus attempts to understand his present nature by moving the past which brought it about into an imaginary future and culmination which the whole process will generate. But as imagination extends his consciousness in time all he can discern is the same continuing, defining unity of perfect love, and so when he concludes that 'the gain of earth must be heaven's gain too' (st. liii), the value of the 'gain' is delicately ambiguous.

The poem comes to suggest then the ironies of idealised love in the context of mortal existence. The dissolution of the present within a temporal expansiveness simply highlights the irony of a timeless and mystical union ('mixed at last / In spite of the mortal screen'; st. xlvii) conceived within the bounds of a temporally confined consciousness, for the success of a perfect union on earth transforms mortal life and eternal life into one continuing stasis, continuity without the regeneration of change. By projecting an act of recall into an imagined future, the speaker discovers not a new self, but a self made and defined by the past which will still be made and defined in that way in the future. His identity is fixed by the passive syntactical patterns of his own experience and by his conception of a moment of ecstasy which determines all thereafter. The only potential freedom lies in the implicit detachment of consciousness in its role as observer, in the air of mild bemusement which expresses a desire to think it all over 'One day' (st. liii); but the passivity of observation contains its own trap of inertia, and the hints of self-persuasion and the underlying doubt are not articulated, for to do that would be to endanger 'the whole', to question the value of perfection itself. Therefore the reverie hovers between a narrative which provides the reassurance of inevitability and a temporal perspective which evokes doubting wonder about how a moment so brief has determined a process so endless. Despite the sense of freedom from present actuality, the expanded perspective which is achieved through conflating memories of the past with imaginings about the future, the irony for consciousness is that it remains poised between the two, fixed by its very awareness of a relationship between memory and expectation.

The construction of memories in 'By the Fireside' illustrates the powerful defining function of time in consciousness. In 'Any Wife to any Husband' a similar demonstration is achieved, although now in terms of the future, through the conditional structures of possibility. The speaker in this poem, the wife, is quite sure that while she and her husband are together his love will be constant, but she fears that once she dies his attention will stray. What hurts is that he would love her, were she there:

> Shouldst love so truly, and couldst love me still
> A whole long life through, had but love its will,
>   Would death that leads me from thee brook delay.
>
> (st. i)

But she is trapped by her subjunctives, in a sense hurt by syntax, prevented by the continuing flow of hypotheses from feeling fulfilment and satisfaction in the present. She does not doubt her husband's ability to value chance and brief events; indeed, 'If old things remain old things all is well' and 'hadst' he only heard or seen her casually, 'not so soon . . . would such things fade as with the rest' (st. vii). But the very fixed nature of their love leads her to doubt him, since he would be able to take for granted its permanence. She dramatises his argument, providing him with rationalisations which would lead him to other women (sts. x–xiii), and she is aware too of the irony that she virtually guarantees his unfaithfulness by these very projections: 'So must I see, from where I sit and watch,/My own self sell myself' (st. xiv). In the last few lines she attempts to rest content within the assurance of his present love, but inevitably she cannot. This poem is not a narrative in so far as it does not tell a story, but it is still concerned with temporal organisation, being dominated by a fearful hypothesis, by feelings which are defined and restricted through the grammar of future possibilities.

A variation of the use of narrative for self-dramatisation, the epistolary method, has already been well described by Park Honan.[6] Discussing 'Cleon' and 'Karshish, the Arab Physician', Honan observes how Cleon treats Protus as an objectification of his own worldly success, and points out that through 'the epistolary framework . . . Karshish is able momentarily to objectify and to transfer his inhibiting professional characteristics' (p. 163). Karshish transfers the scientific facet of his character to Abib, leaving himself, or another part of himself, free to express the religious feelings which are released in him by his meeting with Lazarus. There is, as Honan suggests, a 'delicate relationship' between speaker and auditor, or between Karshish's medical professionalism, fictionalised in the form of Abib, and his less rational excitement about the Christian message. This relationship emerges quite directly late in the poem when Karshish examines his own writing, demonstrating how the letter becomes a means of self-scrutiny:

> Thy pardon for this long and tedious case,
> Which, now that I review it, needs must seem
> Unduly dwelt on, prolixly set forth!
> Nor I myself discern in what is writ
> Good cause for the peculiar interest
> And awe indeed this man has touched me with.   (ll. 283–8)

Thus the awareness of his strange emotion struggles against his scientific detachment which demands a recognisable system of causation before a reality is established. In the postscript his excitement is momentarily uncontained: 'The very God! think, Abib; dost thou think?' (l. 304). But in the juxtaposition of imperative and question the conceptual conflict remains. Amidst the shattering challenge of an 'All-Loving' God, he still describes

Lazarus as a 'madman', which follows his medical identification of Christ as a 'learned leech'. Karshish is indeed debarred from assent by intellectual caution,[7] although it is perhaps closer to the psychological conflict to say that his understanding of his experience is restricted by his inability to escape from the formulations of his scientific self, his inability to describe Lazarus or Christ in terms other than medical or to analyse his reactions in terms not governed by causal principles. The point is not to treat this predicament as a warning against similar offences, but to observe the drama of conception in a man who is fascinated by feelings and thoughts which are continually thwarted and transformed by the conceptual framework of his medically influenced language.

IV

The methods of dramatising the self associated with narration are largely private, projections made in terms of personal experience or manipulations wrought in the context of some inner self-consciousness, even though they may be addressed to another person. Some methods, however, are less directly introspective, involving a greater concern with public roles. Lippo Lippi, for example, has a public identity thrust upon him and it is that which attracts attention, requiring defence:

> Though your eye twinkles still, you shake your head –
> Mine's shaved,–a monk, you say–the sting's in that!
>
> (ll. 76–7)

It is a role in which he is uneasy. At odds with his natural vitality and threatened by several frustrations, it is largely maintained through the contrivances of an energetic self-consciousness. From an early age, Lippo Lippi was required by the necessity for survival to observe human responses closely, so that his impulsive outbursts and abrupt intrusions are accompanied by a watchful awareness of their effects. When he lets slip an unspiritual oath ('Hang the fools!'), he is quick to reassert the monastic monk: 'That is – you'll not mistake an idle word/Spoke in a huff by a poor monk' (ll. 336–7). He is troubled, then, by an uncertainty of self-conception, by the deceptions which emerge from circumstances where natural desire conflicts with public expectation:

> As it is,
> You tell too many lies and hurt yourself:
> You don't like what you only like too much,
> You do like what, if given you at your word,
> You find abundantly detestable.   (ll. 260–4)

The main conflict arises from his dual identification as painter and monk, for his life is marked by the constant battle between his naturalistic art and his Prior's demands for spiritual conceptualising: 'Your business is to paint the souls of men' (l. 183). It is a struggle between the desire for self-expression and the requirements of institutional authority, between his instinctive delight in the world (ll. 313–15) and the Prior's request for formal didacticism (ll. 316–19), and the whole affair has continually frustrated his painter's integrity: ' "Rub all out!" Well, well, there's my life, in short,/And so the thing has gone on ever since' (ll. 221–2). The cost to his identity may be measured by the strength of his anger when, despite the friendship of Cosimo of the Medici, the 'heads shake still' and he is told he will never equal Angelico and Lorenzo:

> So, I swallow my rage,
> Clench my teeth, suck my lips in tight, and paint
> To please them – sometimes do and sometimes don't.
>   (ll. 242–4)

With the new patronage allowing him to be his own master and paint as he pleases (l. 226), this seems an unnecessary submission, but it indicates the depth of Lippo's conceptual dilemma; he cannot separate painter and monk, finding it necessary to sustain the ambivalence.[8]

In this instance, however, inner disharmony and its frustrations are seen to be a source of vitality, for as Lippo endeavours to gain some perspective on himself he holds the contending elements together through a series of energetic dramatisations. The self-consciousness of his posing is a means of indulging and simultaneously distancing from himself those aspects which might not conform to public requirements, and if the histrionic quality of this method leaves the impression of a character whose central focus is elusive, he is nevertheless dynamic, someone whose personality remains rich through the same histrionic methods which enables him to sustain so many facets. There is the endearing urbanity of his beastliness: 'You understand me: I'm a beast, I know' (l. 270). It is a deliberate self-abasement operating in relationship to his public duty, since the image of rogue acts in the context of his monasticism. In the fiction of the proposed painting in the last section of the poem he dramatises another favourite part, the amazed and misplaced innocent (portrayed earlier through recounting how he became a monk):

> I, caught up with my monk's things by mistake,
> My old serge gown and rope that goes all round,
> I, in this presence, this pure company!   (ll. 366–8)

Against such posed naivety he represents a more self-justifying facet of himself through the angelic girl who praises his function as the scene's creator (ll. 373–7). Then, with a self-effacing blush he slips back into his ebullient roguery. He expresses this with the flippancy of a contrived pose (ll. 378–87), but associated with his enthusiasm for 'life's flash' the implicit dismissal cannot mask a real impulsiveness. The histrionic elusiveness of the whole process is what enables Lippo Lippi to resolve the public and private equation: 'And so all's saved for me, and for the church/A pretty picture gained' (ll. 388–9). It has been suggested that the weakness of the dawn light indicates his failure to integrate monastery and street into one vision,[9] but I think his aim is to maintain the factions rather than fuse them into an indistinguishable unity. As he leaves the watch with an ambiguous imperative not to fear him – neither of him nor for him – the implication is that he has survived the test of the night. The poem is about the interaction of inner awareness and public persona; through manipulating dramatised impulses, the speaker sustains the vital coherence of a multifaceted personality.

If Lippo Lippi finds public expectation constantly at odds with his natural responses, another liturgical character, Bishop Blougram, exists quite confidently within the security of his episcopal role. Whatever the merit of Blougram's argument,[10] the poem is still the portrayal of action in character and the bishop's conception of himself provides an underlying impetus. He displays himself to Gigadibs, his sceptical auditor, as a man who has deliberately acquired a public position which satisfies his inner nature, adopting beliefs to need:

> I know the special kind of life I like,
> What suits the most my idiosyncrasy,
> Brings out the best of me and bears me fruit
> In power, peace, pleasantness and length of days.
> I find that positive belief does this
> For me, and unbelief, no whit of this.   (ll. 234–9)

Possessing an agile mind with a keen sense of irony, Blougram is consistently aware of the effects of verbal ambiguity, so that, as David Shaw observes, 'by displaying the duplicity of every thought, he can hold conflicting ideas in balance'.[11] In terms of his personality, this means sustaining a balance between self and role. Just as his explanation of faith and doubt is based on their dialectical interdependence, his self-conception rests on an interrelationship between desire and function.

The argument is based on realistic self-appraisal: there is a 'will to dominate' in him, and he *needs* power and respect (ll. 322–9). And he admits the inevitable artifice: he must 'take what men offer', but do so pretending he would not if it could be avoided (ll. 330–1). Artifice, though, is necessary. The bishop's uniform is imposed upon him by social requirement, not through his choice, but it is through this artificial symbol that the fusion of private and public identity takes place: 'now folk kneel / And kiss my hand – of course the Church's hand' (ll. 335–6). 'My' hand does not seem to me a revealing slip which is hastily retrieved; rather the whole statement operates as a provocative conjunction of individual attribute and social sign, the correlation of person and institution which is basic to the Bishop's view of himself. Thus he is 'made', and thus 'life is best' for him (l. 337). Such a view assumes, of course, the given nature of both self and society. He must affirm acceptance of himself as he is, avoiding the Christian duty of submission to God's will in order to attain new birth, but accepting God's creation as God made it:

> My business is not to remake myself,
> But make the absolute best of what God made.   (ll. 354–5)

Hence he also accepts the world as it is and argues frequently for observing life's realities, through his well-known cabin image (ll. 100–43), or through his concern to seek ease in 'this world', unlike the traveller who is always dissatisfied because always thinking of the next place before leaving the previous one (ll. 780–800). Not constrained by the past and not troubled by the future, Blougram defines his existence in terms of the present, the *status quo*.

He is essentially an empiricist for whom demonstrable achievement is everything. 'How one acts' is his 'chief concern' (ll. 812–13), and therefore the value of life must reside in the moulded image, in what he outwardly shows forth:

> I act for, talk for, live for this world now,
> As this world prizes action, life and talk.   (ll. 769–70)

He judges everything in terms of power and social influence, and assumes, wrongly as it turns out, that Gigadibs does the same:

> In truth's name, don't you want my bishopric,
> My daily bread, my influence and my state?   (ll. 903–4)

Gigadibs' implicit idealism and concern with personal truth suggest that he wants to probe behind this public mask, whereas Blougram meets him with a confidently posed and highly refined self-consciousness which explains how role and man are related, but which still withholds intimacy, because of Blougram's continuously superior attitude. Whatever the skill of his logic in refuting Gigadibs, its aim is to destroy Gigadibs' identification with idealism and assert in its place his own identification with the realities of power. By finally offering an introduction to editors in Dublin and New York, Blougram emphasises his auditor's inferiority, the fact that they have not met equally or openly, and thus flaunts his life's product, embodying his own identification.

Ironically, the success of Blougram's chosen persona denies him the freedom which Gigadibs is able to exercise by emigrating to Australia. Gigadibs makes a fresh start,[12] but Blougram's justifications bind him to the cultural prestige which Gigadibs finally rejects. While the bishopric may provide Blougram with power of action, for instance, it does not give him freedom of expression. He could not talk to his chaplain, he points out, as he has done to Gigadibs: 'My shade's so much more potent than your flesh' (l. 932). By this he means simply that even his shadow is more powerful than a mediocre journalist, but the shadow is his own outline, the chaplain 'reflects' himself as he says, and so Blougram cannot express his doubt, 'the grand Perhaps', to his chaplain because his image must be undisturbed. The irony is that his power is manifested not in himself but in his episcopal function; it is that which must be sustained and therefore that to which he is tied. One difficulty of judging the limits to Blougram's perception is that he is usually conscious of such ambiguities, and in a sense he has already acknowledged this implicit servitude when alluding to himself as God's slave. He claims that needing a God before he can be or do anything is a matter of recognising his instincts (ll. 845–7), but in wanting 'the true thing', no abstraction or 'mere name', he transforms God into the tactile reality of another social relationship: 'a relation from that thing to me, / Touching from head to foot' (ll. 849–50). No longer perceived as an independent spiritual entity, God is thus absorbed into the bishop's balancing of self and role, a concept used to enhance the public context and justify commitment to it. The bishop's whole self-conception, therefore, is of someone who only exists in the self-image which is made through social contacts. It is a definition, however, which is ultimately a conceptual limitation, since its focus on 'fruit' and its dependence on what is given inhibit the possibility of change or growth; Blougram is consequently both identified and restricted by his conservatism, not questioning the hierarchy of privilege which supports his position, devoted to preserving the conditions which sustain his status (ll. 869–71), and unable to conceive any other possibility for himself than a social performance which is justified through the abstractions of a dialectical synthesis. That the synthesis may also be a self-defeating compromise is not something he is required to consider, for his security is never really threatened, partly because Gigadibs is not a political force sufficient to challenge his reputation, and partly because of his own mental processes. In terms of personality, one of the consequences of the poem's conceptualising is that Blougram, through focusing on the reality without, is not required to confront the reality within.

His method includes the provision of metaphors which dramatise himself as a man of reason, practical and realistic, but these images simultaneously evade his inner life, the prospect of emotional or spiritual reality. His contrast between faith as waking life and unbelief as night life, for example, clearly diverts attention away from inner experience, parodying idealism as merely a fanciful concern with dreams which logically should lead to a life spent in bed (ll. 250–65). Similarly, his cabin image is a perfectly satisfactory expression of his empirical identity and an argumentative refutation of the absurdities in idealistic extremism, but it is not an answer to questions about value which would concern the purpose and direction of the journey as well as the accommodation en route. Like so many of his metaphors it dramatises the importance of pragmatic synthesis, but avoids the issue of spiritual realisation. However, if he is therefore a victim of his own argument, he is a willing victim because always aware of the nature of his commitment – the role it requires and the comfort it provides. His images are consciously elaborated, unlike Childe Roland's projections, for instance, and thus demonstrate the shaping power of his rational mind, the authority not of Christian belief, but of a sophisticated self-consciousness. Little escapes the control of Blougram's synthesising attention, which is why Browning required the additional perspective of an epilogue. But it is mental control. It was his 'mind' which the bishop rolled out (l. 978) and his intellectual fluency, which so easily handles the journalist's scepticism, tends to remove any direct sign of his own emotion. One of his main points is the tug of war metaphor: 'when the fight begins within himself,/A man's worth something' (ll. 693–4). But there is little sense of conflict in Blougram himself; the soul's struggle between God and Satan is for him an intellectual image rather than a reality of sensibility. He even approaches an admission of this poverty of feeling when he allows that he would be beaten by the intensity of zealot, poet or statesman – 'Their drugget's worth my purple' (l. 942). Emotionally, he is engaged only on the level of hurt pride, stung because Gigadibs despises him,[13] and his deepest self is therefore not touched, as the poet's epilogue reveals: 'certain hell-deep instincts . . . He ignored these' (ll. 990–4). He is an example, then, of the intellectual whose very facility with language enables him to manipulate his conception of selfhood in order to avoid the pitfalls of any deeply threatening trauma.

V

'Fra Lippo Lippi' and 'Bishop Blougram's Apology' involve examples of dramatisations which are conceived in relationship to publicly determined roles. Another method of self-conception is to focus on a particular topic or person: for instance, the Bishop of St

Praxad's tomb, Caliban's god or Mr Sludge's spiritualism each act as a reflexive identification of the speaker concerned. I should also distinguish between topics which are clearly of special interest to the speaker, closely related to his life, such as Andrea del Sarto's wife or the student's grammarian master, and those which dramatise a separate point of view, one not obviously the speaker's, such as the aged male poet in 'Dis Aliter Visum' or Venetian society in 'A Toccata of Galuppi's'.

Lucrezia's function as a symbol for certain aspects of Andrea del Sarto has already been suggested by Park Honan and more recently by Fred Kaplan, who views her as a personification of the death of Andrea's creativity.[14] As the model for his work she is the continuing muse for his art, though she is an ambiguous muse who delimits as well as inspires, with her physical presence circumscribing as well as stimulating his imagination: 'You smile? why, there's my picture ready made' (l. 33). He paints her as she is, binding his art to her reality, to a literalness of perception and a mundane materialism; had she given him a soul (l. 118) or urged him to pursue idealistic aims beyond the merely material (ll. 127–31), he might have succeeded, he thinks. But there are nuances to what she symbolises which are more various and more broadly suggestive of his character than the one aspect of his creativity. In so far as Andrea is caught between the sterile perfection of her image in his painting and the emotional reality of her lack of understanding and responsiveness, Lucrezia is also a means of indicating how his limited imagination is related to the essential stasis of his self-conception. That connection is suggested, for instance, when in discussing the buoyant years in France he reveals his fear of the very success he desires. As Lucrezia grew restless, wanting to leave, his instincts agreed since their life, he says, had grown 'too live' (l. 168). Regarding himself as a bat which is troubled by the sun's brightness, he is unable to imagine how he would survive amidst the excitement, particularly not without Lucrezia: 'How could it end any other way?' (l. 171). Instead, he returns to the 'home' of her heart, projecting onto her another facet of himself, his desire for the peaceful protectiveness of a domestic cliché, and that need is evinced several times in the poem as he attempts to persuade her to stay with him for the evening. Further, if she is a muse whose physical presence has become obsessive, she is also a consolation for being less than Raphael; possessing the reality is the excuse men will make for him when they observe that the Virgin of his art was his wife (ll. 177–80). And he also transforms his craving for public acclaim into her need for persuasion about his merit; it is she who must hear the judgement when he paints just one more picture in France (ll. 231–3). Above all, however, Andrea's relationship with Lucrezia reveals the crippling irony of his basic ambivalence. This is evident from the beginning where his dilemma is embodied in the very structure of his address: 'Sit down and all shall happen as you wish' (l. 3). The imperative is linked directly with its consequence, so that Andrea is only able to command through the promise of capitulation – self-assertion for him is self-defeat.

The literal marriage to Lucrezia means psychologically that Andrea is wedded to conceptions which ensure his failure, although this irony is not the main source of his anxiety; rather it is that in possessing the beauty of her image, he also possesses a reality which compels him to recognise his illusions. Unlike Fra Lippo Lippi or Bishop Blougram, he is unable to identify with a successful public persona. He knows there is no real consolation in Lucrezia, that she is not 'more pleased' because he gave up his chance of artistic success for her. 'Well, let me think so' (l. 203), he says, acknowledging his need to believe in her. He knows too that his hopes for future success are merely fictions, and he expresses his willingness to pay for the 'fancy', if only Lucrezia will sit with him and allow him to 'muse' on the one final picture he would paint if he were back in France (ll. 226–31). Andrea finds this awareness difficult: it threatens his desire for well-being, conflicts with other impulses and prevents him from settling into any satisfactory pattern of existence. Any attempt at resolution ends in linguistic contradiction (ll. 49–52, 132–5) or the evasion of a platitude (ll. 252, 257). But he must find a point of rest or allow his self-respect and with it his coherence as an individual to perish, and in this predicament the deepest irony for Andrea is that Lucrezia is indispensable. He can fancy painting one last picture of someone else, but he cannot imagine doing it without her there to hear the judgement (ll. 231–3). His final insistence that he will always fail because there will always be Lucrezia may seem like a startling and unnecessarily masochistic commitment, but in context it is inevitable, and the climactic action of choosing this situation (l. 266) is the crucial act in the poem which defines and cements his ambivalence.

To claim choice in this way is to claim that the self is made, not something given or discovered. Andrea implied the same principle earlier when suggesting through his passive syntax how external events were imposing his autumnal melancholy, his youth and art 'being all toned down' to 'sober Fiesole' (ll. 39–40). By describing that scene 'as if' he saw himself as a 'twilight-piece', he retains a detachment from the image which still allows other possibilities for himself (see Chapter 1 above), but at the end of the poem, recognising that possibilities no longer exist (even in the future he will be 'overcome'), he commits himself to this act of self-creation. The difference is in whether identity is involuntarily determined by outside forces or consciously shaped from within, and Andrea has been trapped earlier between two opposite conceptions: the man who cannot be responsible for his life because he is fate's victim, and the man of will who governs his own destiny and who may yet attain success (ll. 132-40). The first is inadequate because he still wants to believe in possibility, and the second is unsatisfactory because it leads immediately to his limited aesthetic vision and deeply rooted timidity. As the monologue ends the second alternative seems to collapse altogether, since his perception of the reality which Lucrezia represents means he is no longer able to believe he could be other than he is, and yet he clearly feels the need to exercise his will as if he could. In claiming freedom of selection in a situation where he can no longer imagine alternatives, he continues the ironic contradiction which he has always expressed about determinism and free will, but he also dramatises a deeply felt urge to maintain the image of a self-determined identity, to maintain, as I have suggested, the coherence and unity of his individuality. This image is of course a fiction, for Andrea is characterised more by his indecisiveness than by conscious will, but it is a fiction which has a complex function. While it means submission to Lucrezia, acceptance of failure and self-betrayal, it also means assertiveness and self-determination, or in other words consciousness of being. Andrea's 'choice' is an impulsive reaching for self-validation, a histrionic act which by representing a stasis of personality ensures its continuity.

We are faced with the paradox that while the relationship with Lucrezia is emotionally tenuous, even painfully so, it is the continuity of this relationship which sustains Andrea, enabling him to avoid the dissolution of consciousness which is threatened every time he attempts to resolve his uncertainties. In choosing Lucrezia he embraces the ineluctable self, admitting that he cannot free himself from his own crippling attributes. He also commits himself to a relationship which dramatises and so objectifies his faults; the

faults are thus distanced from himself, and he is able to escape a
direct encounter with what is so potentially dangerous to any self-
conception at all – the inner chaos of doubts, fears, hopes, desires.
He selects an existence with someone for whose nature he cannot be
held responsible and by choosing *her* he is able to avoid having to
'choose' himself, for that is a creativity Andrea is unable to achieve.
His creative inadequacies govern his character as well as his
painting. Only because he chooses Lucrezia, therefore, can he make
any choice at all, and yet at the same time it is no choice, because he
must stay with her or face the perils of self-creation. Of course his
choice implicitly claims that he does make himself, but again the
paradox is that it is only choosing Lucrezia which sustains such an
illusion. His very failure with Lucrezia also, ironically, provides the
value in this paradoxical act. If she were more responsive, fulfilling
his domestic fiction, for instance, there would be less reason to
blame her; the 'choice' would be less daring, less assertive and
therefore lack some of the force of its self-affirming function. Indeed,
without *this* Lucrezia, Andrea would need to invent another,[15]
although rather than manifesting Andrea's death wish as Kaplan
suggests (p. 105), she is a means to keeping alive his sense of
selfhood. This choice is existentially inauthentic, but psychologically self-sustaining.

Browning rarely suggests the importance and psychological
subtlety of choice as overtly as he does in this poem. Here it is no
simple self-deception, but an act which is necessary to the survival of
consciousness, and it is an act which can only be achieved verbally.
As much as any Browning poem 'Andrea del Sarto' indicates the
essential function of language in the process of self-conception, and
in doing this Browning seems to take the implications of *Pippa Passes*
to their ultimate conclusions; that is in terms of the need to think we
make free choices in order to maintain the illusion of an independently generated consciousness. The verbal statement of
choice for Andrea may commit him to failure but at least he does
something, effects the necessary fiction which hides the void of
disintegration until next it threatens. The final command of 'Go, my
love' is not simply a gesture of surrender,[16] but another verbal
enactment which combines self-assertion, in the imperative verb,
with self-capitulation, in the commitment to a mere illusion of
fulfilment by addressing Lucrezia as his 'love'. The gesture is
histrionic, a posed confidence, and it is a language act whose
meaning is essentially personal; since it has no substantial function

in the referential world – Lucrezia will leave regardless and she is
neither 'his' nor his 'love' in any real sense – its function is mainly
psychological. Dramatisations or the histrionic potential in language were for Lippo Lippi the demonstration of continuing
possibility, but for Andrea del Sarto they are merely the means of
maintaining a stasis, of constructing the fiction of an articulated
identity which is necessary for any consciousness of self at all.

The shifting tones of Andrea's monologue and the dominance of
his relationship with Lucrezia form the focus of a conceptual
conflict which dramatises his centre of consciousness; this conflict
and the ambiguities surrounding his choice contribute substantially
to the fictional reality of his character. In 'A Grammarian's
Funeral', a student's account of his grammarian master, the
speaker's concern with his subject is an equally important means of
identification, but the student exhibits far less self-consciousness
than Andrea and instead of conflict about self-conception or the
rigours of active choice, there is an unthinking absorption in what is
seen as the grammarian's idealism. With this there is effectively a
dissolution of individuality in the ideal, so that the student is not
defined by the degree of particularity which distinguishes characters like Andrea or Fra Lippo Lippi. Rather he takes on a
representative quality, assuming the collective identity of the
grammarian's disciples – 'Let us begin . . . singing together' – and
it is perhaps this diffusion of the speaker's personality which has led
to a general focus of attention on the grammarian instead.[17]
Nevertheless, the poem portrays an act of conception whereby the
grammarian's views are not presented directly, but dramatised in
terms of the speaker's perspective.

That perspective is illustrated by the way an outward literalness
forms an ironic counterpoint to the grammarian's metaphysical
idealism. As the procession moves from the dull 'bosom of the plain'
to the 'rock-row' which is 'the appropriate country' (ll. 5–9), the
speaker's purpose is dominated by what constitutes 'the proper
place' for the burial (l. 133). This physical action is a strong
element in the poem; it is continually present in the student's
consciousness and it is underlined by the rhythmic incongruity
between the long iambic pentameter and the alternating abrupt
combination of dactyl and trochee. In this context, praise of the
grammarian begins to act less as a formal eulogy and more as a
justification for burying him on the mountain, and this implicit aim,
combined with the student's awareness of the watching public (ll.

25–6, 73–4, 76), becomes part of a subtle intrusion of material issues into idealistic abstractions. In so far as the grammarian's philosophy meant a renunciation of the flesh and a focus on the soul's reward (' "Hence with life's pale lure!" ', l. 112), it should hardly matter where his tomb is located, but it clearly matters to the student–speaker who defines the right place through a literal-minded symbolism of meteors, clouds and stars (ll. 141–3). Through the funeral he pursues a physical goal which would demonstrate literally the grammarian's superiority:

> Loftily lying,
> Leave him – still loftier than the world suspects,
> Living and dying.   (ll. 146–8)

It is as if he seeks a special status in the world for the grammarian despite the grammarian's more heavenly aims, and in this the speaker begins to use his master's idealism to aggrandise his own status, for it is really the student's elitism, in ironic contrast with the grammarian's selflessness, which he expresses: the thorpes are 'vulgar' (l. 3), the plain is 'unlettered' (l.13) and the multitude live below 'for they can, there' (l. 138). Perhaps some of this is merely the natural reaction of a piqued devotee annoyed by the world's indifference to his enthusiasm, but it does indicate the role of his perspective in the poem, and how that perspective underlies and shapes the oration.

In an address which contains many exclamations and rhetorical questions, the student is never far from the histrionic, and movement between the expressive and the dramatic is often indicated by shifts in emphasis or the fluctuating quality of his language. Consider, for instance, the passage which introduces the goal of the procession:

> Seek we sepulture
> On a tall mountain, citied to the top,
> Crowded with culture!   (ll. 14–6)

As successive phrases lead to a climactic exclamation, the sentence moves beyond description of the burial place into a dramatising of the student's excitement about human culture; embodied in the attraction to a crowded city, such enthusiasm hints at the mixing of social aspiration with funeral solemnity. In a similar example of shifting tone, the ritualism of the 'Hail to your purlieus' passage (ll. 134–6) is immediately followed by the contrasting casualness of 'Here's the top-peak; the multitude below/Live, for they can, there', and the supercilious assumptions in that remark make the histrionic posturing of the previous lines even more obvious – a rhetorical flourish appropriate to the 'proper place'. There are other ways too in which the language is demonstrative of the speaker's bias. Some images are clearly designed to aggrandise the grammarian: he is apostrophised as beginning life with the appearance of 'Lyric Apollo!' (l. 34), and later he attacks his studies 'Fierce as a dragon' (l. 94). As suggested by the comic incongruity in that image enthusiasm is inclined to overcome discretion, leading in one instance to a looseness of expression which exalts the grammarian but with the unintentional irony of doing so at God's expense: to 'throw on' God the burden of finding a use for learning (l. 101) makes the act an offhand affair which treats God as merely an extension of man's work, man's servant who will fill in the necessary gaps. Rhetorical questions are not always rhetorically convincing, often dramatising without justifying. Did not the grammarian 'magnify the mind, show clear/Just what it all meant?' (ll. 105–6). Hardly, and certainly not when God has to complete the. meaning of his work. The logical ineffectiveness of many of these expressions mean they serve mainly to express the students' idealisation of their master, and that is also revealed in the dominating dramatic technique of contrasting the grammarian with the world (ll. 39–46), what he would say with what others would say (ll. 55–64, 81–4). These juxtapositions effectively polarise his idealism against the world's doubt and timidity, portraying his philosophy as a heroic uncompromising commitment: 'He ventured neck or nothing – heaven's success/Found or earth's failure' (ll. 109–10). But the effect of this method is not just to highlight an idealistic gamble, it is to separate achievement from intention. Although the students record their master's devotion to scholarship, what is eulogised is his hypothetical life rather than his actual life:

> Oh, such a life as he resolved to live,
>   When he had learned it,
> When he had gathered all books had to give!   (ll. 65–7)

It is the grammarian's grand purpose which is celebrated most, as in this epigrammatic absolute: 'This man decided not to Live but Know' (l. 139). Earlier statements, however, make the result less than absolute – he was a man 'with a great thing to pursue' who 'Dies ere he knows it' (ll. 115–16). His aim was apparently to 'Image the whole, then execute the parts' (l. 69), but the complete design was always left to God and his actual tasks were to do with the small particulars, *'Hoti's* business' and 'the enclitic *De*', seeming rather to reverse the claim, examining the parts before envisioning the whole. Thus the students idealise their master through interpreting the meaning of his life in terms of its intention rather than its reality.

The combined action of march and eulogy dramatises the students' view of their function: to carry an ideal through a dull, uncomprehending world to lofty peaks of ritualistic grandeur. In one sense their master was more realistic, since while he lost sight of the end of his work, he did what was immediately practicable. But for the students the realistic is associated with dull, sleeping villages and what is more important for them is that their journey is the embodiment of a coincidence of the grammarian's aims and their own, of his steadfast devotion and their cultural elitism. His life was heroic as he 'grappled' with the world (l. 45), continued despite baldness and leaden eyes (l. 53) and strove with death's 'throttling hands' (l. 125), and this daring is echoed in their own action as they leave the protection of crofts and thorpes, 'Safe from the weather!' (l. 30), braving the narrow path (ll. 90–1). The students reach their goal, fulfilling *their* intention and ending with feelings of satisfaction and triumph, but that intention (to bury their master on the mountain crowded with culture) is directly related to their interpretation of the grammarian's intentions, and thus the concluding action of reaching the mountain top is a manifestation of what are for them indistinguishable aims: scholastic idealism and cultural success. The symbolism of the place is in accord with symbolic meaning of the grammarian's life, since the triumphant tone at the end of the poem celebrates not the man himself or his achievement, but what he represents. By the end of the funeral any individuality he once had has disintegrated into a 'rattle' and 'stammer' and been transformed by his students into 'lofty designs'. How he conceived of himself we cannot know; the inference is that he increasingly lost any sense of either self-consciousness or purpose

through an absorption in scholarly minutiae. No doubt
C. C. Clarke is right to say that the grammarian's 'monomania is
both noble and absurd', and that 'we are not to be allowed to make
a conventional distinction between the ludicrous and the
sublime',[18] but to emphasise that sort of judgement is to avoid the
more basic dramatic quality of the poem, which like other
monologues is to be found in the way the act of shaping perception is
immersed in fluctuating processes of language and in the manipulations of a self-defining consciousness.

In 'A Grammarian's Funeral', as in 'Andrea del Sarto', there is a
close relationship between the speaker's character and the discussed
object of his monologue, but in poems where the speaker dramatises
a point of view not his own that relationship is obviously less
intimate, leaving the reflexive element of the discussion less direct.
Although an objectification of self still operates, it does so through
having the imagined viewpoint provide another perspective on the
speaker. Shaping or repeating someone else's argument is a step
towards multiple perspectives, but since the monologue form makes
the projections monistic, they are more the multiplicity of a protean
personality than the conflicting views of social interaction. The
speaker places himself within a mesh of perspectives where he must
somehow locate his identity and in this, naturally, there are varying
results. To explain the action of another may be to justify a superior
attitude, though it may also lead to an awareness of deficiencies and
weakness; it may be to accommodate feelings of loss and disappointment by turning them into a momentary moral triumph, or to
discover that the multiplicity of perspectives dissolves into the
emptiness of a cold centre. Such differences are illustrated variously
in 'Dis Aliter Visum' and 'A Toccata of Galuppi's'.

The female speaker in 'Dis Aliter Visum' extends her perspective
by dramatising a poet's rationalisations when he prevented himself
from falling in love with her. In the poem she has met the man again
ten years later and it seems he has just related his version of the
original meeting. She repeats his thoughts, thrusting them back as a
challenge: 'Stop, let me have the truth of that / Is that all true?'
Browning does not allow us to know whether she reports the poet
exactly, but on the assumption that the arguments are coloured by
her own phrasing, what is implicitly dramatised is her own view of
the poet's limitations and anxieties. She controls at least the context
overtly and by prefacing the representation of his argument with
repeated questions about whether he had really thought that way,

she undermines both his attitude and his reliability. He is shown to be vain and fickle, but above all apprehensive, afraid of the aftermath to passion and of spontaneous commitment, holding back through the machinations of a speculative consciousness. Clearly she sees him otherwise than he sees himself, blaming him for thwarting her fulfilment and for missing the opportunity which would have saved four lives (they have both subsequently married), but the title, dis aliter visum (seen otherwise by the gods),[19] implies a broader perspective even than hers and the reader may see 'otherwise' again. Her report of the poet's reasoning is designed as a mirror in which he might see himself, but it is a double mirror, reflecting herself as well.

The woman's emotional investment in the lost chance is suggested by the wealth of remembered details which she adds to the account and by the obsessive intensity with which she follows the poet into labyrinths of temporal hypotheses, his projection of what might occur if they did marry, his speculation about her thoughts then (ll. 73–85) and his reply to those thoughts (ll. 90–100). But she had little evidence for the reciprocation of her feelings: it had been only their second meeting (l. 11), outwardly the poet said nothing other than pleasantries about their surroundings (ll. 101–7), there was a large age difference between them and a gap in cultural experience, since he was already a known poet when they met (l. 158), whereas she was a novice in art (ll. 14–20). Such differences did not trouble her (ll. 133–5), and through a series of rhetorical questions she suggests that she anyway was ready to commit all for love and eternity (ll. 116–29). But in this she places herself among the boys for whom love is life or death (l. 81), and the whole affair takes on the appearance of a young girl's fancy, now turned bitter with passing years. Even the original moment was not a mere chance in her eyes, but the manifestation of God's purpose: 'WHO made things plain in vain?' she asks (l. 112), and she adds to the failure of their love the 'despair' of God's failure (l. 130). The poet, then, has not only thwarted her, but the whole providential plan – a presumption which suggests the strength of her romanticising. Social opinion reinforces her interpretation, as 'all say' that the poet's wife danced 'vilely' – 'her vogue has had its day' (ll. 148–9). This waning success acts as a claim that the social attainment and aesthetic companionship which the speaker thinks the poet sought when he rejected her have done him little good, but it also functions as an assertion of her righteousness: events have proved her right, she and the poet were lovers whose destiny he destroyed. This dramatised version of the poet's reflections of a decade ago brings the speaker no new self-knowledge, but it substantiates her view of herself as someone who missed the god-given moment for grand passion, a martyr to someone else's timidity, fickleness and excessive rationalisation. By objectifying his attitudes in order to indicate their limitations, she sustains her own self-conception, largely by avoiding the possibility that his view may have contained some justice. In other words her perception of him is a function of her conception of herself. By turning present frustrations into moral superiority and jealousy into spiritual vindication, her drama-tisation of the aged poet's mind is a means of accommodating acute disappointment and the painful dream of a once possible eternity.

If the female speaker in 'Dis Aliter Visum' is unaware that she is dominated by a private obsession, the speaker in 'A Toccata of Galuppi's' is more self-conscious, and Galuppi's music functions for him as a mask which represents his own self-questioning. Dramatis-ing the expressive qualities of the music is a means of gaining self-knowledge, but that is knowledge finally of participation in a larger mutability and here understanding the self becomes an ironic process of disillusioning the self. However, the poem not only records that process, representing what happens as the speaker listens to the music, it also expresses a detached consciousness, the speaker's awareness of a more general condition which is embodied in the continuity of his relationship with Galuppi. Stanza xi, for example, encapsulates both his immediate predicament and the enormity of its continuing recurrence:

> But when I sit down to reason, think to take my stand nor swerve,
> While I triumph o'er a secret wrung from nature's close reserve,
> In you come with your cold music till I creep thro' every nerve. (ll. 31–3)

The speaker is a man haunted by the toccata and what it means to him. It is 'like a ghostly cricket, creaking where a house was burned' (l. 34); not allowing him to build any certainty or belief, it torments him by reflecting his own sense of doubt and ephemerality. The music's statement (ll. 35–44) objectifies his attitude of superiority over the self-indulgent Venetians and reinforces his desire for immortality: ' "Butterflies may dread extinction, – you'll not die, it cannot be!" ' (l. 39). But the music's tone is ironic, implying the fiction of his 'triumph' over nature, and through the agency of the toccata and the perspective on himself which it brings, the speaker becomes essentially the victim of his own irony.[20]

He assumes a number of voices in the poem: the chiding, wary speaker in the opening lines who knows what the music means and 'all the good it brings' (l. 4); the voice of imagination which responds 'as if' it saw all (l. 9); the desires of musical harmonies (ll. 20–2) and their implicit indication of Venetian frivolity; a social satirist and Victorian moralist (ll. 25–30); a Venetian socialite (ll. 26–7); and the music's main expression (ll. 35–44). In so far as several of these voices portray views outside himself he remains apparently detached, but increasingly they incorporate him with them, leading him to confront the loss not only of soul or the soul's immortality, but also of the 'gold' which was the hair of beautiful Venetian women, to observe the value in the sensuality he disdained. As the music objectifies the reward of 'mirth and folly', the fruit for Venetian society 'here on earth', and hints at the ultimate futility of human endeavour which ends in 'dust and ashes', the speaker is aware that he too is part of this sensual process, that the consciousness which seems detached is itself absorbed, and he is struck finally by the depth of loss involved. The dramatisation of the music and its effects is a measure of his self-consciousness, and the conflicting impulses are embodied in the conflict between the toccata as a piece which is normally a virtuoso display – sustained in the poem through Browning's perpetuum mobile rhythm which consistently repeats the quaver-like quadruple motif of a rapidly flowing toccata – and the underlying sense of emptiness and transience which brings only a 'heavy mind'. Unlike the Venetians who could admire Galuppi's superficial brilliance without further penetration, the speaker's own doubt finds too much of a sympathetic reflection in the music's harmonic implications to remain unmoved. The poem records the epiphany wrought by the toccata, though it is an epiphany which is immersed in its own repetitiveness. It is a dispelling of illusion rather than a release into revelation, the representation of a condition of mind rather than a discovery of truth. The final remark is no longer histrionic, though neither is it merely a statement of feeling: 'I feel chilly and grown old'. In this moment of devastation the speaker combines expressiveness and consciousness, his definition of feeling and the realisation of a condition. The word 'grown' demonstrates his awareness of a transformation, of an inexorable process which brings the desolation of experience, and the consciousness is an actuality, an existential state, not some hypothesis based on conditional language. In this instance, histrionic possibility has brought the speaker to an awareness of a bleak coldness at the centre of being.

VI

It is clear from the preceding examples that in Browning's poetry self-dramatisation appears in a variety of circumstances and involves a variety of methods, although my main intention in identifying this phenomenon is to indicate the central locus of Browning's dramatic purpose as it is revealed in the monologues themselves. There we are constantly confronted with man's function as a psychological actor, performing on the stage of his own mind. Certainly social interrelationships are important to many of the poems, and these are usually represented by the interaction of character with auditor, but even these relationships are largely an indication of the speaker's self-portrayal and their ironies a guide to the speaker's subjectivity, as I have argued for 'Andrea del Sarto', 'Fra Lippo Lippi', 'Bishop Blougram's Apology' and 'Dis Aliter Visum'. The isolating, circumscribed focus of the monologue form reinforces an emphasis on the confinement of human awareness and on the transposition of external matters into a self-absorbed mental process. What seems particularly characteristic of Browning's use of the form is the way self-expressive lyricism becomes subsumed into the impetus for self-definition, leading to a use of language for dramatic as well as expressive purposes. The artifice of language in his poetry is indissolubly linked with the action of consciousness, or in his own phrase 'action in character', and consequently such artifice has as much to do with sustaining the values of identity as with performing the skills of poesy.

Browning's art reflects man's capacity for histrionic action, action which underlies an individual's perception of himself, articulating self-consciousness, defining a conception of identity, validating that conception through objectifying it. In this process language is obviously fundamental. The results of dramatising the self are richly various in accord with the range and variety of human experience, but at the same time what seems to be a recurring and challenging implication in the drama metaphor as Browning uses it is that individuality, the sense of a unique consciousness and the self-definition which accompanies it, is a concept which is essentially dependent on the histrionic possibilities of language.

4 The Function of Illusion

It is a main tenet of my approach to Browning that his monologues do not propagate a philosophy, but dramatise a shaping activity, that in particular they formalise the way men use language as a self-reflexive process. Since to dramatise the self is obviously to manipulate an illusion, the poems inevitably raise questions about the fictional dimension of human experience. Whether in terms of the display of a social pose, the emotional necessities of self-deception, the outline of belief or simply the consequences of using language which is metaphoric, illusion is a natural concomitant to the use of a drama metaphor for human existence. At the same time dramatic artifice is itself a reality, and in Browning's hands the monologue becomes a form which implies a basic epistemological question. A feature of his portrayal of 'action in character', for instance, is the ambiguous and usually ironic relationship between the reality which is transformed through the formulations of speech and the reality which is created by the transformation. It is not that this ambiguity renders the speaker's reality a merely distorting illusion; the speaker's vision is a truth nonetheless, but it is a histrionic truth, inseparable from its reflexiveness and from the ironies of its construction.

Throughout Browning's writing the discernment of fictions is an issue. The speaker in *Pauline* began life reading books which were 'All halo-girt' with 'fancies' of his own (l. 320), sought feeling in himself like that which he found in fiction (ll. 578–9), and exclaimed regretfully that the ideal life 'should be but dreamed!' (l. 985). At the other end of Browning's career, Apollo, in the Prologue to *Parleyings with Certain People of Importance in their Day*, admits that 'It seems, then – debarred/Of illusion . . . Man desponds and despairs'. In 'A Likeness' the speaker considers the role of portraits in their owners' lives: his own print is 'a study, a fancy, a fiction' (l. 35), and although it may have no value as an object, being 'only a duplicate'

(l. 68), it embodies for him an ideal, 'A face to lose youth for, to occupy age / With the dream of, meet death with' (ll. 65–6). The picture hints at the power of a mere image, how a singular fancy can evoke and identify feelings which might not otherwise be discovered. In 'Love in a Life' emotion becomes focused not so much on an image as on the elusive abstraction of a quest; it is not physical contact with the beloved which brings life's satisfaction, but an involvement in seeking the real person while being sustained with mere signs of her presence: the perfume in the couch, or the mirrored reflection of her feather. The companion poem, 'Life in a Love', elaborates aspects of the quest, with the speaker admitting that 'the chace takes up one's life' and recording the way he continually shapes a new hope as the old one falls – hope is the self-made goal which maintains his impetus (ll. 16–20). All these poems dramatise the role of illusion in providing the necessary stimulus for pursuing an arduous existence, and they all implicitly question the reality of human experience. What is believed may be a fiction, although nonetheless a real and powerful influence in human affairs.

Frequently, speakers who express a transcendent vision betray at the same time a solipsistic interpretation, a fictionalising of the world where they create their own enriched reality. 'Cristina', for example, records the making of an illusion for satisfactory living. The speaker feels 'sunk' in the dullness of plain existence (st. iii), but a fleeting glance from a beautiful woman inspires him to build on its meaning and erect a splendid speculation of fulfilment. His first remark attempts to turn responsibility for his reaction onto Cristina herself: 'She should never have looked at me / If I should not love her!' By focusing immediately on Cristina's intention, he is able to assume both the reality and purposefulness of her glance; yet it is precisely these assumptions which are at issue, threatening his belief:

> What? To fix me thus meant nothing?
>   But I can't tell (there's my weakness)
> What her look said!   (st. ii)

Despite this admission, his response is to transform the uncertainty into a theory of significant moments, sudden insights which bestow a supreme value on existence, 'When the spirit's true endowments / Stand out plainly from its false ones' (st. iii), and through this account the threat of contingency in a chance event is absorbed into a theoretical framework which emphasises meaningfulness and purpose. But he ignores the epistemological question he has already acknowledged. How are these moments to be known or judged? It can only be through their effect upon him, and the subjectivity of his response is what he barely rationalises. His evidence for Cristina's intention is merely the demanded affirmation of a rhetorical question: 'Doubt you', he asks, if she felt that the 'true end' of the soul's time on earth was 'this love-way' (st. v)? And while he recognises that she returned immediately to the 'world's honours', he explains this lapse as simply the devil's work which extinguishes knowledge in order to ruin rapture (st. vii). Such explanations are of course conveniently self-supporting: what *he* knows is divinely inspired ('God's secret'); the lack of understanding in others is caused by the devil. Finally, he solipsises Cristina's image in a vision of acquisitive perfection, relinquishing altogether any concern for external confirmation as he celebrates his own conclusions:

> She has lost me, I have gained her;
> Her soul's mine: and thus, grown perfect,
> I shall pass my life's remainder.   (st. viii)

Like an emotional credit account Cristina's loss is his gain. Through incorporating into his consciousness this illusion of a soul blended with his, he will be able to live on with a sense of completion and purpose. He believes what cannot be substantiated and thus enjoys the emotional benefits of an unacknowledged fiction. What matters for him is not the ambiguity of the perception, but the rewards of the image, a sense of meaningfulness in a life otherwise 'sunk'. In this discovery of the returned flash it does not matter if the reflecting surface was false or even whether it was there at all; what is important is simply his perception that there was a return, a mirrored reflection which acknowledged his hopeful gaze on life giving it meaning and identity: 'Such am I: the secret's mine now!' Language therefore functions rhetorically to lead the speaker to an affirmation of God's secret – now he can know it as his – and the poem is thus a process of self-discovery, an actualising of fulfilment through the artifice of reflexive consciousness.

In 'The Last Ride Together' the speaker similarly pursues the benefits of subjectivity, displaying as he does so another act of conceptual transformation. The last stanza has often been regarded as Browning's noble realisation of a romantic heaven, where two lovers could ride together on,

> With life for ever old yet new,
> Changed not in kind but in degree
> The instant made eternity.   (st. x)

But in context the basis for this vision is merely the vanity of personal desire, since the action in the poem is the mistress' last, reluctant ride with the speaker before she breaks their relationship. Actuality therefore has been transformed into a dream of permanence. 'It is quite clear', as David Shaw observes, 'that the mistress is indifferent; there is nothing reciprocal, and hence nothing real, about his adventure'.[1] Being 'deified' for 'one day more' is an illusion and the final vision is built not even on hope but on the memory of hope, which in the first stanza is all the speaker claims and which is all that is left of his identity as a lover. Having lost real hope, he turns the image of hope, its memory, into a philosophy of immediate action.

It is a sceptical philosophy which places past hopes 'behind' and rejects all teleological goals as intangible and problematic. The account of his ride in stanzas iv to ix is not a description of action at all, but a rationalisation of present experience as the only determinable reality. Through a series of rhetorical questions he undermines the merit in all human endeavour which is based on striving towards future success, hinting at its inevitable disappointment: compare 'This present of theirs with the hopeful past!' (st. v). The technique of questioning of course proves nothing, not even the success of his own riding where being 'together' is a euphemism, but it is sufficient merely to suggest the futility in all striving and in the vicarious nature of aesthetic pleasure, since that allows him to claim his present action as the only substantive value. 'Sing, riding's a joy!' he says to the poet: 'For me, I ride' (st. vii). By organising stanzas in such a way as to end with the statement of his riding, he constantly places the certainty of his action against the uncertainties of seeking after idealistic success. As a result, his consciousness of time narrows its focus, absorbing future ends into present means: if goals were achieved on earth, he reasons, there may be nothing to look forward to in heaven (st. ix). Such a conception may be formulated as a question, but again the posited doubt is sufficient to shift value from consummation to process, and to enable him to state the reality of his situation ('Now, heaven and she are beyond this ride') in the context of a hypothesis which makes that reality a psychological virtue. At the same time the shift of emphasis from goal to action implicitly replaces the reality of the woman with the reality of experiencing her presence. Not the fulfilment of reciprocal love, but experience itself becomes the image which is celebrated, and the speaker has moved the significance of love from shared feeling to personal perception, from the truth of mutual affection to the truth of experienced proximity. The reiterated statement of his riding is thus a verbal act which restores the confidence and value of his own consciousness.

In all this his companion does not speak and therefore does not intrude into the argument, enabling him to move finally into the obvious extension of his philosophy: having extinguished the importance of time past and time future, he is struck by the thought that time present may become absolute. Based on the constructions of possibility, on the hypothesis of 'What if' (st. x), his speech functions more as the expression of desire than as the perception of a transcendent absolute. Nevertheless, even though the 'heaven' he contemplates would be an ironic wish-fulfilment, a solipsistic endeavour because the extension of a self-focused world where the only reality is his belief in the perceptions of a moment, desire can still lead to the excitement of conviction, to an ecstasy of possibility, emotionally poised between past and future, between the value of experience and its illusory basis. The poem thus illustrates perfectly the role of fiction in sustaining a feeling of value in existence even when failure is inevitable; it is the process of transforming emotional defeat into psychological triumph.

In two other poems, 'Evelyn Hope' and 'Too Late', the personae are also faced with unrequited love, partly because their love was never known, and partly because of the more severe problem that the women whom they adore are now dead. Hope is dispelled even more forcibly for them that it was for the speaker in 'The Last Ride Together', but they too develop a personal reality in order to sustain the value of what may be. The speaker in 'Evelyn Hope', for instance, idealises his feelings, transforming them into a per-sonalised cosmic myth. Without an independent object of his love living to challenge the process, he absorbs the girl into his own emotional universe, a universe which is based on belief in God's willingness to create 'the love to reward the love' and where fulfilment is a distant teleological goal. Whereas the previous speaker responded to the challenge of a last ride with his mistress by reducing temporal consciousness to the value of immediate action, this persona, because denied experience in the present, transfers the value of his desire and the reward for his ardour into a future when 'the time will come' (st. v).

Sharp physical details in the opening stanza contrast with the speaker's idealising of Evelyn – the 'pure and true' soul made of 'spirit, fire and dew' (st. iii) – to form a disjunction between material reality and his mythic idealism. Similar contrasts between their age (she was sixteen and he is 'thrice as old'), their social milieu (their paths 'diverged so wide'), and between her youthful inexperience and his devoted absorption ('It was not her time to love', whereas he loved her 'all the while'), suggest a disjunction in his experience which has always threatened the success of his love. Now, however, Evelyn's death has released him from the bonds of probability. A relationship potentially doomed while she was alive becomes ideally and ironically possible now she is dead, when the abstract beauty of her 'sweet white brow is all of her' (st. ii). Hence in this poem the pattern of elegiac reconciliation becomes the pattern of the speaker's own intensive idealism. He is in love with a paradigm rather than an individual and the reality and power of that image lead him to an identification with the constructions of his own belief. In the last stanza, for instance, he places a leaf inside Evelyn's hand:

> There, that is our secret: go to sleep!
> You will wake, and remember, and understand.

But how could she? She is already dead and when alive she scarcely knew his name (st. ii). In Evelyn's world the gesture is meaningless, and yet to the speaker her death has been accommodated into a pattern of quest and discovery, so that for him the act is a physical sign of the spiritual fulfilment to come. For the reader it also signifies his transformation of fact into fancy: the literal leaf into subjective secret. The gesture is a final representation of the speaker's devotion to maiden innocence, to a virginal purity which becomes the idealised mythic goal of all desire, and yet at the same time it indicates the defining emotionalism of subjective perception. Indeed, the excessive nature of a desire which will persevere through several lives, 'traverse' several worlds (st. iv) and eventually have 'Ransacked the ages' (st. vi) is an emotional extravagance which verges on self-parody. While the speaker takes this trans-cendent extension for granted, its pattern is still indicative of the reflexive function of his language. He of course believes what he says, without irony. But he has attached his feelings to a fiction of possibility, given his life meaning by transforming his passion for Evelyn Hope into another kind of reality – a tacit identification with the symbolic illusion of her name.

When the speaker in this poem asks if it is 'too late' (st. iii), his reply emphasises the promise of future fulfilment, but for the speaker in the poem 'Too Late' rewards seem no longer possible and the consolations of illusion more difficult to establish. In 'Too Late' consciousness is not so kind; amidst the painful awareness of disillusionment and its threat to self-definition, personal reality becomes difficult to determine. Even the speaker's physical situation is ambiguous. Certain images suggest that following Edith's death he has committed suicide, stabbed himself perhaps or drunk poison: there is the pulse in his cheek which 'stabs and stops' (l. 10), his whole life 'ends to-day' (l. 39), he 'bleeds' tears (l. 95), there are two who 'decline' and 'enjoy' their 'death' in the darkness (ll. 119–20), and he says finally that he lays Edith's hand to his lips (l. 134), as if joining her in the grave. But the churchyard is 'miles removed' (l. 8), he claims a long life for himself (l. 109), and he asks Edith to bid him 'live' (l. 135). If the last stanza suggests the overtones of some necrophiliac ritual, I suggest they emerge from the speaker's imagination, for Edith is seen standing, not lying (l. 141), he is potentially drunk on wine (l. 142), and he is a man whose life has been dominated by the possibility of action, never by action itself. His life has been defined by the hypothesis that 'time would tell' who was God's choice for Edith and until now he knew that she breathed: 'I could bide my time, keep alive, alert' (l. 108). But now she is dead and the reality of possibility which filled his inner life is exposed as a vain fiction. It is the illusion of purpose which has been destroyed and with it his identity, so that his death is psychological, not necessarily physical. What the poem portrays is his emotional turmoil amidst the uncertainties of conflicting impulses and the desperate desire to salvage something of his lost identity by making love's grand gesture even though it is too late.

The persona in 'Too Late' has always viewed himself imaginatively. He claims that he was the grand lover, the man of idealistic gestures who 'Poured life out' and 'proffered it' with a flourish: '"Half a glance / Of those eyes of yours and I drop the glass!"' (ll. 71–2). He was the rat who 'belled / The cat', the reckless fool who 'got his whiskers scratched' (ll. 75–6), but always in his imagination, for clearly the glass was never actually proffered. He has thus created for himself a schism between aggressive and passive selves. Hitherto aggression seemed still possible, though it has been suppressed, as in the example of the stone, through hypotheses about the way some other agency might act for him (ll. 20–36). Now all aggression would be futile anyway, and all he can do is wreak his rage on 'the empty coat' of the past (ll. 43–6). But this is still imagined violence, the mere image of action, which is what he conjures up as he broods on what he should have done:

> Why, better even have burst like a thief
>> And borne you away to a rock for us two,
> In a moment's horror, bright, bloody and brief.   (ll. 55–7)

In this plethora of alliterative b's he suggests the strength of his desire to be other than he is and the potential destructiveness of his terrible frustration, but it is all dissipated in language, and he knows the role of ruffian would have given way to the passive servant:

> Then changed to myself again–'I slew
> 'Myself in that moment; a ruffian lies
> 'Somewhere: your slave, see, born in his place!'
>> (ll. 58–60)

It is consciousness which is so painful, his awareness of what has been, of failure (ll. 92–5), and of yearning for another chance (l. 97), and therefore it is consciousness which is transformed through the linguistic reality of verbal affirmation in one last effort to sustain the original purpose in his life. In the final stanza he again shapes his role as devoted slave, restoring the force of possibility as he promises Edith, through an accumulation of appropriate phrases, that he shall indeed perform the required task, pay 'Full due, love's whole debt, *summum jus*' (l. 138). In the next breath he restores Edith herself, in a phantasm of sensual simplicity: 'There you stand, / Warm too, and white too'. Confronted with this presence, he proffers one more gesture:

> would this wine
> Had washed all over that body of yours,
> Ere I drank it, and you down with it, thus!

This is the climactic act he wishes could occur: a sacrament of love in which he literally consumes his beloved. It would be the equivalent of Cristina's absorption into a vision of perfected identity, a literal solipsising of Edith equal to that of Evelyn Hope, and yet it remains only a wish, built on another subjunctive. Fulfilment in action, even verbal action, remains as remote as ever for the speaker in 'Too Late', but in the last stanza he turns his back on the world (l. 133), and through the affirmation of language divorced from the control of a referential reality he may still restore an illusion of potential action. He is able to believe at least momentarily in Edith's continuing presence.

The personae in these four poems all respond to a disruption of their emotional security by emphasising their own conceptual process, and the absence of defined or independent auditors allows them to develop these views without interruption, to absorb their conceptions more easily into the structure of their belief. In 'Cristina' and 'The Last Ride Together' the auditors are entirely vague, making the argument in each almost directly between the speaker and himself. In 'Evelyn Hope' and 'Too Late' the auditors are the two dead women and this linguistic objectification of the dead figures, addressing them as if alive, reinforces the illusion of their continuing existence, with Edith in particular being trans-formed from her initial role as the focus for private anguish into the spectral image of a visualised presence. In these poems where Browning dramatises personae who are isolated through un-requited love and lack of physical contact, the reader is able to observe the composing of private realities; for these personae more than most, dependent as they are on their own consciousness, the language of their response is all they have. Experience for them is a process of interpretation which absorbs personal needs and private desires.

However, a monologue which epitomises even more clearly both the solipsising process and the use of language for a mirroring self-reflexiveness is 'Caliban Upon Setebos'. There the argument by analogy of Caliban's natural theology means that his knowledge of Setebos remains but knowledge of his own experience: the act of theological definition is an unconscious act of self-definition, where the illusion of the former defines the realities of the latter. Arnold Shapiro has already observed that 'Caliban presents his god Setebos as the mirror image of himself', that Caliban's speech is 'totally reflexive', leaving him unable to escape 'the prison of self'.[2]

Nevertheless, what requires further discussion here is the ironic
relationship between this specular process and Caliban's self-
conception, particularly in the context of his play with make-
believe.

Caliban's aim is to understand the behaviour of his god in order
to avoid the wrath of his god. Assuming that Setebos is 'Placable if
His mind and ways were guessed' (l. 110), Caliban hopes to find
ways of pleasing him: 'There is the sport: discover how or die!'
(l. 217). Caliban faces the problem of surviving in a world
dominated by chance, where the only rule for pleasing god is that
there is no rule,[3] and where without any covenant between ruler
and ruled there is no restraining morality and no conceivable
purpose except survival and the exercise of power.[4] Caliban's fear
and verbal struggle is indicative then of his desire to exist in the face
of what he perceives as an overwhelmingly destructive principle,
and his attempt to explain Setebos, the threatening force, is
essentially an attempt to use the rationalisation which language
affords as a means of imposing order on lawlessness and
contingency. The structuring process of language may give some
sense of control within the chaos of sensation and feeling, but the
order which Caliban produces is of course an ironic circularity
which discovers only himself. The metaphors which form the basis
for his argument by analogy emerge from his own sensory
experience, so that he constantly equates sensation with thought, or
feeling with abstract perception, and through this confusion he
transforms his own pain, fear and jealousy into the animus of a
natural power, the deity who explains their existence. Caliban does
not conceptualise so much as project his experience, and through
always attributing his vexation to an external cause he remains
unaware of the implications in his method, that he might be the
source of his own misery. Because his conscious mind is locked in
sensory experience, controlled only by the structure of its analogical
argument, Caliban cannot transcend his own unconscious impulses,
and because he remains oblivious to the reflexiveness of his
argument the shock of self-recognition remains outwardly directed
as the shock of Setebos' apparently sudden return (ll. 284–91).

In this situation Caliban's self-awareness is clearly limited, but
that does not mean it is lacking altogether. Of Caliban's third-
person references, a feature of the poem, David Shaw says they are
'a sign that he cannot even identify himself' (p. 194), which is true if
by identity is meant some consciously expressed, coherent self-

definition, since Caliban's self-references tend to be descriptive rather than analytical, a perception of what he does but without understanding. However, Caliban's use of the third person is complex. Not only may it be a device for avoiding responsibility for whatever action might bring wrath upon him, it may also be seen as an attempt at objectivity, a means of distancing his own experience so that his evidence for Setebos' nature has the appearance of objective empiricism. By holding up his experience before himself in the mirror of retold or hypothetical events which this use of language provides, Caliban is able to observe the nature of that experience and therefore of himself. Of course Caliban, despite the potential for self-knowledge in this process, transfers the image to Setebos, directing his attention outwards instead of turning it introspectively inwards. Thus he does not develop an awareness of internal selfhood because he looks instead to an external 'He'. In order to attain an understanding of his existence which would enable him to reconcile the conflicting demands of survival (or fear of destruction) and fulfilment (or desire for self-assertion), he defines that existence in terms of a god who is both its source and its destiny. In the power and freedom of Setebos he sees both a threat to his survival and the possibility for fulfilling potential, and in the continual equation of his own attitudes with those of Setebos is the identification of himself with his god.[5] The equation emerges from the recurring phrases of transference, 'so He', and also from moments when through sudden shifts from Him to him the antecedents for the pronouns blur and merge in an ambiguous mélange of self and other:

> 'Saith, He may like, perchance, what profits Him.
> Ay, himself loves what does him good.   (ll. 179–80)

> You must not know His ways, and play Him off,
> Sure of the issue. 'Doth the like himself.   (ll. 224–5)

In the literal sense of identity as oneness Caliban does, then, identify himself through third-person devices, not directly as an act of self-definition, but indirectly through an ambiguity of references. In this, of course, Caliban's consciousness remains limited. While aware of the transference, he seems unaware of the reflexiveness, but for the reader this confusion of Him and himself becomes the solipsistic conflict of an ego struggling to survive the threat of its own destructiveness.

Caliban's self-conception is more clearly indicated in passages where he does use the first person. They occur mostly in moments of authority, where he exercises a cruel power over his subordinates and where he equates his own arbitrary wilfulness with Setebos; he says of his action towards the crabs, for instance, 'As it likes me each time, I do: so He' (l. 108). The first person also occurs in moments of vexation: 'He hath a spite against me, that I know' (l. 202). In these passages Caliban identifies himself in terms of capricious power, whether as perpetrator or victim, and a similar preoccupation emerges from an even more important conception when he dramatises himself as his own slave, an imitated Caliban:

> This blinded beast
> Loves whoso places flesh-meat on his nose,
> But, had he eyes, would want no help, but hate
> Or love, just as it liked him: He hath eyes. (ll. 181–4)

In the condition of the sea-beast who has been deliberately blinded by Caliban, he embodies his perception of himself as the victim of a tyranny greater than his own and in need, therefore, of a freedom greater than his own: Setebos has eyes and consequently the choice in love which the sea-beast (and Caliban) lacks.

The crucial quality which Caliban identifies is the freedom to act at will: ' 'Doth as he likes, or wherefore Lord? So He' (l. 240). Yet this is how Caliban would be and where Caliban's aspirations begin to forge a trap for himself, since reliability in his eyes becomes thence a weakness which would limit freedom and circumscribe authority. Setebos must be capricious, in Caliban's view, or otherwise succumb to a self-imposed law which would allow others to define him through expectation, thus making him not Lord (ll. 232–40). In that proposition, however, Caliban denies the one principle which might provide the security he seeks – the divine covenant which is implicit in Browning's allusion to Psalm 50 in the epigraph.[6] Caliban places himself in the ironic position of having his psychological need to define Setebos contradicted by his conception of Setebos as morally indefinable. Any definition is of necessity an outline of limits, so that Caliban's conception of limitless freedom undermines his analytical purpose. In seeking a principle of order and to escape from fear, he predetermines his failure at the point when he confuses freedom with licence and when he cannot conceive of power as other than an exercised, demonstrable tyranny.

Caliban of course feels the constraint in his own situation, and his obsession with his own limited power underlies also the function of illusion in the monologue. Since he is his own auditor, with no-one else to hear, his desire to vex Setebos by talking about him is a sham (ll. 15–19).[7] But that irony is part of Caliban's whole play with make-believe, and it is consistent with the ambivalence between his assertive impulse which would flaunt his own nature and his fearful self which would seek protection from outside threat. He is continually histrionic, making for instance a grand challenge in calling out Setebos' name (l. 24), although since he is sure Setebos is away for the summer his incantation is merely an act, a mock challenge. Caliban exhibits all the comic ostentation of a pantomime, but dramatising his actions, whether as fanciful possibilities (ll. 75–94), present action (the crabs 'march now', ll. 100–8), or memory (ll. 192–7), is a means of exercising his power without hindrance, of developing the passing illusion of a freedom equal to that of Setebos. Hence part of his performance is to imitate Prospero, the other dominant figure in his life (ll. 150–69), gaining a vicarious pleasure in aping Prospero's authority. Although Caliban ultimately feels cheated because the role is not a reality, the fiction of 'make-believes' provides solace, for without the prospect of unrestricted action all he has is the pretence of absolute despotism; and its value, as for the imitated creativity of making a totem (ll. 192–9), rests not in the fact of the illusion or in the object which is made, but in the pleasure which is felt through the making. The role of pretence also provides Caliban with a strategy of deception: 'Even so, 'would have Him misconceive, suppose / This Caliban strives hard and ails no less' (ll. 263–4). He proposes to appease Setebos through a ceremony of mock contrition (ll. 271–8), and his parade of histrionic gestures has become finally a means of finding some suitable role for survival. His sacrifice in the last lines is essentially therefore an 'act' which would deceive Setebos and thereby gain an implicit power even over the deity.[8] Caliban's fear may be genuine, but his contrition is a matter of appearances. What he does not recognise, however, is that deceiving Setebos is merely deceiving himself, and hence the ironic link between illusion and self-definition: Caliban's attempt to achieve a secure identity through make-believe and pretence condemns him to the tyranny of his own self-conception. His stumbling efforts to reason the nature of his god, using language which is tied closely to the record of sensation, reinforce the illusion of a substantive reality, the reality of both a referential deity and a referential self, Caliban; but the ability of language to reflect also the cruelty which Caliban transfers to Setebos means that he is all the more imprisoned by his analogical method.

The ugliness of Caliban's vision has led many critics to suggest that Browning intends the reader to perceive goodness and perfection through confrontation with their opposite. David Shaw, for example, argues that Browning brings men to God 'by first driving them apart' (p. 202), thus making the poem a form of disguised evangelicalism where the reader is led to belief because of an unpalatable hell which is the alternative. But this view assumes a pre-existing pattern in human responsiveness, where men who are confronted with an unpleasant extreme will replace it with an attractive opposite. Through Caliban Browning evokes fear of an irrational, chaotic world, and this kind of critical response seems less concerned with the poem's portrayed action than with an un-acknowledged desire for a moral order which bestows meaning beyond randomness and purpose beyond being. Rather than a satire of any particular human belief,[9] 'Caliban Upon Setebos' is a general parody of human subjectivity. Without revelation, natural theology is man's epistemological condition, and Caliban's ironic self-imprisonment is therefore a grotesque parody of all mono-loguists: the frightening spectacle of man as an isolated actor making his own despotic hell without knowing it. Despite the measure of comic vitality in the image, its cruelty is of course crudely repellent to any sensitive feeling, and notwithstanding any unwilling fascination which may be evoked for amoral and self-destructive instincts, it is understandably easier and more pleasant to read the poem as the intended affirmation of an antithetical benevolence. But that would be to ignore our own emotional investment in the interpretation. Caliban's unwitting parody of rational understanding is, I think, the essence of Browning's solipsistic monologuists, and discussion of this poem, more than of any other monologue, absorbs the reader's consciousness into that solipsistic circle. Despite the many attempts to escape Caliban's web through the paradox of meaningful opposites, the readers of this poem seem constantly to illustrate the way Browning may draw attention to subjectivity but without taking us out of it.[10] Critical empiricism is by no means a guarantee of hermeneutic objectivity – not even, alas, for myself.

II

In the poems discussed so far in this chapter the fictional dimension of a solipsising process has been a persistent theme. For most speakers the reality of belief, however much the product of private conceptualising, has been a source of emotional satisfaction, even psychological survival, and the reflexiveness of their reasoning is an irony for the reader which does not diminish their illusion of success. Even Caliban thinks he may have the measure of an oppressive power greater than his own. Yet he, like the others, remains oblivious to the infusion of fancy as he strains to shape a personal truth, that ambiguous reality which may be at once a delusion and an actualising of potential.

For some of Browning's personae, however, fiction is a more conscious affair. Cleon, for instance, clearly knows the difference between fancy and fact, and consequently, like a more refined version of the distraught speaker in 'Too Late', he is painfully aware of how much can be proposed in the mind but not achieved in action. Although identifying himself with the progress of Greek culture, effecting in his achievement a synthesis of all the arts (ll. 61, 139–46) and dramatising himself in terms of horticultural refinement to stand as the consummation of all human development (ll. 147–51), he remains acutely disappointed, burdened by the ironies of consciousness. Evolutionary progress in knowledge has brought to Cleon an accompanying awareness of limitation and failure: man is torn between the cravings of the soul and the fatigues of the flesh (ll. 239–50). Notwithstanding pride in his success, he feels betrayed by the poet's dilemma of knowing that action expressed in art 'as though' it were his own is but an illusion (ll. 285–8). Thus, as he points out that Protus should not confuse 'knowing how' with 'actually living' (ll. 281–3), he separates the fictions of consciousness from the realities of existence. It is a distinction with disturbing consequences, for he is tormented on the rack of paradoxes: caught by the way the very breadth of his imaginative vision demonstrates the poverty of his experience, and tantalised by the way his desire for joy increases while his capacity for joy decreases. The irony for the poet who recognises the fictional nature of his imagined experience is that there is no reconciliation between illusion and actuality, since the older he grows the more they diverge. Cleon cannot relate the fancy of creative potential to any fact of realisation.

He is a realist, then, for whom the reality of being exists only in the phenomenal world, and so he identifies himself in terms of the demonstrated achievement of his works. Protus' list of what Cleon has done combines with the evidence of improvement through cultivation to objectify his cultural success: it is there to see, part of human reality. While he dismisses as 'a dream' his imagined 'fiction' of a god who revealed the unified purpose of human experience (ll. 115–27), his identity as the synthesis and pinnacle of Greek culture is a fact which emerges from what is 'no dream', the reality of organic development. He stands himself as the 'better flower' of cultural refinement (ll. 147–51), so that while his physical existence may be ephemeral his status is independently established: 'I pass too surely: let at least truth stay!' (l. 157). There is a matter-of-fact confidence in this remark which is part of Cleon's general tone of objective detachment, his academic method of parenthetical phrases and subjunctive clauses, and there is a protective element to the intellectual control which through the logic of understanding masks him from the worst effects of his sense of failure. At the same time this implicit separation of organic being and cultural definition, supported by intellectual discernment and the apparent reality of experience, is the germ of a schism in his consciousness which increasingly threatens the very unity which constitutes identity. It is the dilemma which reveals itself finally in the horror of impending death:

> When all my works wherein I prove my worth,
> Being present still to mock me in men's mouths,
> Alive still, in the praise of such as thou,
> I, I the feeling, thinking, acting man,
> The man who loved his life so over-much,
> Sleep in my urn.   (ll. 318–23)

The 'I' who lives will die, while the physical embodiment of himself, his works, the achievement which identifies that 'I', will live on. That is a devastating irony, a paradox of consciousness which consciousness can barely tolerate, when the reality which establishes identity will mock an obliteration of the consciousness which knows it has been established. The dilemma arises from consciousness itself, from Cleon's discrimination between potential and actuality and from his belief in the objectivity of his own cultural definition, so that the source of his horror lies ironically in the very constitution of his character. 'It is so horrible', he says, that he is driven to do what he considers extraordinary, to 'dare . . . imagine' some possible solution, an act which seems daring because an irrationality, a mere fiction forced on him by 'joy-hunger' (ll. 323–8). But as excitement about its possibility starts to grow (ll. 329–31), the logic of his identity reasserts itself and he falls back on his cultural assumptions with a gesture of disappointment, restoring sanity with an academic subjunctive:

> Zeus has not yet revealed it; and alas,
> He must have done so, were it possible!   (ll. 334–5)

Behind the subjunctive lies his evolutionary assurance that all which could happen has happened. He thus subverts his own projections of a new possibility through a combination of cultural and intellectual superiority, and in the same way he dismisses Christian teaching. Brought by 'a mere barbarian Jew', it is a 'doctrine' which 'could be held by no sane man' (ll. 343, 353). He has already rejected his own story of an incarnate god who revealed himself to men, and although Cleon badly needs another perspective from outside his consciousness, he remains blind to its value when it comes since he finds little to distinguish it from his own fiction. Believing from his knowledge of fictions that a separation of imagined potential and actual being is the necessary product of civilised consciousness, he can find no credence in an uncivilised source which proposes otherwise, and certainly not in the interdependence of spirit and flesh required by any doctrine of incarnation.

We are left with the irony that Cleon's very understanding makes him a closed personality, and with the larger irony that he cannot see this as also a fiction, his consciousness as itself an idealism emerging from the articulation of his conflict. To objectify himself in the language of his letter is to make a self of whom he can be conscious. He *is* therefore his own explanation, shaping his nature through his formulation of stress and his refusal to believe in fancied possibilities. It is the same irony of solipsism which dogged Caliban, alleviated here only by the outside reinforcement of Protus' letter, and even that is absorbed into the argument and assumptions of Cleon's self-conception.

The paradoxes of limitation arise in 'Cleon' from a recognition of
the difference between illusion and phenomenal reality, but in 'Mr
Sludge, "the Medium" ' Browning creates a character for whom
such boundaries are deliberately blurred. A young medium's tricks,
for instance, are described as embellishments, as decoration rather
than fabrication:

> Strictly, it's what good people style untruth;
> But yet, so far, not quite the full-grown thing:
> It's fancying, fable-making, nonsense-work –
> What never meant to be so very bad –
> The knack of story-telling, brightening up
> Each dull old bit of fact that drops its shine.   (ll. 188–93)

Such a passage is typical of Sludge in its array of apparent synonyms
and accumulation of explanatory phrases which tend to obfuscate
rather than clarify; it is rarely his concern to discriminate carefully
among meanings, but rather, unlike Cleon, to affirm the am-
biguousness of possibility. In this manner he develops a plea for the
real Sludge, the man as distinct from the medium, and an apologia
for illusion.

In the first part of the poem Sludge shifts responsibility for his lies
from himself to his patrons. They do his business for him, responding
to his acts in terms of their own predilection to believe and generally
transforming what they see into their own truth (ll. 308–9). In this
context Sludge portrays himself as the unwilling dupe of social
impetus. His patrons demand progress (ll. 407–16), and he is
powerless to resist: 'there's no avoiding fate' (l. 419). This image of a
predetermined plot cleverly diminishes his own culpability, although fate here means social expectation rather than providence.
Like any competent showman he provides what the public wants.
His psychic manifestations are therefore characterised at this stage
of the argument as the embodiment of hopes, confirmations of desire
or mirrors for belief. If his performances are an illusion, they are
simply an appropriate reflecting of the public's self-deception, and
as the creator of illusion he places himself among other purveyors of
fiction: what he does is 'Really mere novel-writing of a sort, /
Acting, or improvising, make-believe, / Surely not downright
cheatery' (ll. 427–9).

At the same time, while that may be how he identifies himself, he
knows it is not how he is identified by society, and this buoyant
cynicism is accompanied by an underlying and deeply felt

grievance, for while admitting his tricks and that he is named 'Cheat' (l. 430), he is also galled by the title. Sludge's dilemma of self-conception emerges from the way his conformity to social expectation means he has submitted to social definition, become identified by his function instead of his individuality, and in accepting the role required of him he bitterly resents the de-personalisation and moral label which accompany it. To others he is merely 'the medium-pane', the window to another world (l. 325), the 'drudge' for spirits (ll. 335–8); he is reduced to the ranks of 'hysteric, hybrid half-and-halfs' and 'worthless vermin' who 'yield the fire!' (ll. 567–8). Sludge consequently writhes within emotional ambivalence, caught in a hypocrisy which becomes his own psychological trap. He may secretly scorn the conceit of his patrons and feel angrily insulted by their destruction of his humanity – he is treated 'as a showman's ape' (l. 600), as 'only the kind of thing / They must humour, fondle' (ll. 612–13) – but outwardly he is expected to be grateful for their solicitude. He has been paid for a play, but what was bought was more than an actor's skill: 'my soul you buy!' (l. 650). This is an obviously extravagant protest, and yet it is an appropriate focus for his anger and frustration, since the role of medium makes special demands on his talent which challenge the survival of his individuality. He cannot just pretend to be Macbeth or play tricks in his own name, 'Sludge as Sludge' (ll. 651–6), but must obliterate and deny his separate self, actually becoming the new persona. What he conveniently ignores is that this situation develops because he claims to provide a reality; it is his function as medium which requires that he should *be* Macbeth and not *act* Macbeth, and so Sludge's sense of individuality is at odds with the public role which he professes to play. In him Browning portrays the victim of a role-playing irony: someone who knows he is the dupe of fools but who cannot say so without shattering the necessary image. It is a conflict which is sustained throughout the poem, although for the moment Sludge dissociates self from mask in one defiant dismissal of the whole business as a theatrical artifice:

> Enough of it all! I've wiped out scores with you –
> Vented your fustian, let myself be streaked
> Like tom-fool with your ochre and carmine,
> Worn patchwork your respectable fingers sewed
> To metamorphose somebody, – yes, I've earned
> My wages, swallowed down my bread of shame,
> And shake the crumbs off – where but in your face?
>
> (ll. 657–63)

That is, the real Sludge merely performed as expected, wore a clown's uniform and acted out somebody else's perception of a metamorphosis.

From this point, Sludge develops what is in effect an elaborate discussion of the value of lies or fictions in a social context .where illusion characterises everything. There is even, he claims, 'a real love of a lie' (l. 694), and his world is a society of self-seekers and hypocrites who continually use him to enhance their own designs: opportunists without any belief at all who act as 'promisers of fair play' (l. 740), literary men who half believe in order to sell their books (ll. 751–3) and who transform unsavoury 'muck' into 'artistic richness' (l. 757), and social sages looking for a doctrine to use as 'a chopping-block' in order to prove their own wit (ll. 776–9). Amidst this exploitation of his social mask and general web of duplicity he seeks his own truth:

> This trade of mine – I don't know, can't be sure
> But there was something in it, tricks and all!
> Really, I want to light up my own mind.   (ll. 809–11)

Since Sludge is by now receiving tea (or coffee) and sugar (l. 797), and is therefore no longer required to appease Horsefall, it is likely he means to be genuine here, even though integrity for him is rather a matter of wits and superiority than moral rectitude. Although the working out of his need to know what he is tends to be a process of diminution, the struggle to reduce everything to its lowest common denominator in order to establish himself as at least as valuable, there is in this a will to survive, a desire to establish his own reality within so much ambiguity. Sludge's argument for value in what he does is therefore an argument for value in himself, and the two concerns are never really separate, despite his earlier distinction between self and role. It is quite consistent, then, that his image of experience should be directly solipsistic, with everyone else assigned to the position of spectator within a fairground illusion:

> My care is for myself;
> Myself am whole and sole reality
> Inside a raree-show and a market-mob
> Gathered about it: that's the use of things.   (ll. 908–11)

There follows from this belief his perception of the universe as a

maze of signs which instruct him in God's purpose. Even the
minutest phenomena are omens for his benefit: if the white pigeon
flies off first he will confess (ll. 971–6), or if the left pip falls off first he
will leave the trick alone (ll. 1034–7). He proposes an absolute
determinism which in his view makes the world his servant and
natural events a guide to his every step. His whole attitude exhibits
the comedy of travesty – Hamlet's providence in the fall of a
sparrow becomes for him 'a providence in the fire's going out' (l.
962) – and the plausibility of a zealous consistency. But the irony is
that *he* is the slave, to exigency and to his own imposed alternatives
(he, after all, defines the signs). The self-importance which he feels
through being the centre of a universal code of instruction is also a
denial of his own will and freedom, and he is the ironic victim
therefore of his own egotism, trapped and impoverished by his role.
Sludge becomes caught in the paradox that to defend the value of
his spiritual fraud is to deny himself the respect of a self-determining
character. He claims that he absorbs all – 'I'm eyes, ears, mouth of
me, one gaze and gape, / Nothing eludes me, everything's a hint' (ll.
1013–14) – but this self-conception reduces him to the level of
unreflecting absorption, the 'window-medium' role he resented
earlier, or the stomach-cyst which he calls the simplest of God's
creatures – 'mouth, heart, legs and belly at once' (l. 1119). The
reductionism of his method redounds also upon himself.

Sludge's emphasis on the meaning to be found in chance is also
the basis for his whole reliance on possibility. Ultimately nobody
can know whether spiritual phenomena are true or not and his
apology relies frequently on a verbal torrent and confusion which
blurs the crucial issue of epistemology:

> It's all absurd, and yet
> There's something in it all, I know; how much?
> No answer! What does that prove? Man's still man,
> Still meant for a poor blundering piece of work
> When all's done; but, if somewhat's done, like this,
> Or not done, is the case the same?   (ll. 1015–20)

The mixture of rhetorical questions, melodramatic gesture, obvious
truism, cynicism and apparently genuine reasonableness serves to
erase the distinction between acceptable fact and unacceptable
absurdity, and his method is based on the constant appeal to
inconclusive evidence. He continues, for instance, with a statistical

hypothesis:

> Suppose
> I blunder in my guess at the true sense
> O' the knuckle summons, nine times out of ten, –
> What if the tenth guess happen to be right? (ll. 1020–3)

But how he determines the success of the tenth summons is never considered, and this argument is rather like saying that a clock which does not work gives the correct time twice a day. The statement may be logically correct but is functionally useless. Indeed it is typical of Sludge to proceed on a series of movements from speculation to the assumption of certainty, from a requested concession (l. 833) to claimed 'fact' (l. 1215). He is ready to transform the hypothesis of 'what if' (l. 1022) into the quasi-aesthetic assumption of an 'as if', characterising, for instance, coincidence and the inexplicable as gold amidst 'the dirty rest of life' (l. 1216), and then turning that metaphor for value into truth itself. Even then his vision is expressed in terms of epistemological elusiveness: 'Truth questionless though unexplainable' (l. 1220).

In the last 250 lines of the poem Sludge provides three principal justifications for his lies: illusion is a means to truth, illusion is a means of transforming the world and fulfilling all desires, and illusion is merely the stock in trade of all story-tellers and artists. In each instance he advances an undeniable property of fiction, but at the same time he neglects the crucial paradox that fiction may only function as a truth for as long as it is known to be a fiction. His argument that a lie is a means to truth rests, for example, upon the way an image simulates reality:

> If I should lay a six-inch plank from roof
> To roof, you would not cross the street, one step,
> Even at your mother's summons: but, being shrewd,
> If I paste paper on each side the plank
> And swear 't is solid pavement, why, you'll cross
> Humming a tune the while, in ignorance
> Beacon Street stretches a hundred feet below. (ll. 1293–9)

But the paper is only a device, a simulacrum of pavement; if he mistook the image for reality and walked on the paper *as if* it were pavement, then quite a different result would ensue. While he deals with possibility Sludge cannot be refuted easily, but when he attempts to shift from the conditional to the substantive, he performs a sleight of hand which is the verbal counterpart of his spiritual conjuring. He admits that his transformation of the world is an act of deliberate make-believe, the slap of the 'harlequin's paste-board sceptre' (l. 1392), and he justifies that through the value it brings, the 'happy consequence' of 'Each want supplied, each ignorance set at ease' (l. 1400). But this joyful wish-fulfilment – 'What would you have? Just speak and there, you see!' (l. 1406) – is the same kind of solipsistic absorption that characterised the speaker's perceptions in 'Cristina', 'The Last Ride Together' and 'Too Late', and the nature of the experience as a convenient pretence rather than a rewarding metamorphosis is unwittingly suggested when he describes its transcendent aura:

> all half real,
> And you, to suit it, less than real beside,
> In a dream, lethargic kind of death in life,
> That helps the interchange of natures, flesh
> Transfused by souls . . .   (ll. 1415–19)

By turning 'death in life' into an 'interchange of natures', Sludge suppresses the required self-deception in favour of an ecstatic self-exchange, thus avoiding the observation that 'death in life' might be something to do with loss as well as gain. He proposes a happy interfusion of fact and fancy which would have all the appearance and therefore the benefit of 'flesh / Transfused by souls', but the point at which the 'bubble' may burst, when the bliss of illusion may descend into the despair of reality, is quickly set aside: 'if you nearly see / The real world through the false, – what *do* you see? / Is the old so ruined?' (ll. 1421–3). In Sludge's image of 'the Golden Age', illusion is rather a means of transformation than of revelation, an evasion of harsh truths rather than their embodiment, and for that purpose the reality of the histrionic must be asserted while its artifice is suppressed. Thus, when referring to the fictions of poets and authors Sludge emphasises their subjectivity: 'Each states the law and fact and face o' the thing / Just as he'd have them' (ll. 1446–7). But he ignores the way writers acknowledge the artifice of their subjectivity through the very nature of their product – a book is a metaphor for truth, whereas a seance purports to be the thing itself. Sludge 'acts the books they write' (l. 1442), but neglects to observe

that the nature of the artifice in the two activities affects whatever
status he claims for the fiction which results.

Finally, this tendency to confound distinctions between the
reality of an image and the reality of a substantive fact has ironic
consequences for Sludge's character. As I have already observed, he
is faced throughout with a personal paradox: the fulfilment of his
role as medium is a functional denial of the fulfilment of his
individuality, for in acting as a medium he is purporting to become
other than himself, and if he is to defend that claim then he has to
face its consequences in terms of his identity.

> I tell you sir, in one sense, I believe
> Nothing at all, – that everybody can,
> Will, and does cheat: but in another sense
> I'm ready to believe my very self –
> That every cheat's inspired, and every lie
> Quick with a germ of truth.   (ll. 1320–5)

Inherent in this expression of concerned doubt is his psychological
need to believe. He knows he cheats, and without belief in what he
does he, his 'very self', is no more than a sham; he must believe in the
potential truth of his acts in order to restore at least the illusion of a
self-respecting identity. This pose of honest ambivalence is therefore
both a display for Horsefall's benefit, part of Sludge's successful
escape from public exposure, and an assertion of what he calls his
'very self' as having substantive existence. However, as a monologuist who is a spectator at his own performance, Sludge also places
himself among the market-place observers of his own 'raree-show',
requiring himself to observe his own sham production, the manner
in which he is a consummate actor, always adopting the pose
required of him – and therefore never being himself. When he plays
upon the image of a child he asks what is implicitly his habitual
question – 'How shall I act a child's part properly?' (l. 1143) – so
that his whole personality is a continual pretence, the parade of
whatever mask is required by the circumstances, and his character is
thus as much a manipulation of artifice as his play with spiritualism.
There is no real self, therefore, only the fiction of a series of enacted
roles, accompanied by a consciousness of their effect. Underneath
lurks not a self-determined and rounded personality actualising the
potential variety of its nature, but merely the disgruntlement of an
ill-shapen ego which is angry at being caught cheating, and that is

amply demonstrated in the concluding lines when he is shown making up another pose to present to the world – this time one which will dishonour his challenger, Horsefall.

> I too can tell my story: brute, – do you hear? –
> You throttled your sainted mother, that old hag,
> In just such a fit of passion: no, it was . . .
> To get this house of hers, and many a note
> Like these . . . I'll pocket them, however . . .five,
> Ten, fifteen . . . ay, you gave her throat the twist,
> Or else you poisoned her! Confound the cuss!   (ll. 1505–11)

III

In his implicit claim that illusion characterises all human perception, Sludge observes the transforming process of mind which Browning so often dramatises. At the same time, while such an observance allows Sludge to challenge the idealising self-deceptions of his critics, the vigour and tenacity of his pursuit imply an obsession with the folly of others which blinds him to the deceptions of his own position. Combined with other limits to his understanding, such as the way the paradox of truth in falsehood becomes in his hands a parade of histrionic truth which suppresses its artifice in order to emphasise the fruits of its reality, this blindness means his monologue also represents the potential maze of irony and ambiguity which may be produced by that transforming process. Still, Browning assigns to Sludge a fecundity of imagination which, even if self-destructive in its deceptiveness, is self-sustaining in its creativity, and the vitality of human imagination and its capacity for transmuting a drab world is not only a theme but a source of incredible richness in Browning's poetry.

Browning clearly portrays the ambiguity in man's fiction-making potential, the delights as well as the dangers, the possibilities for fulfilment as well as for fraud. The illusions of self-conception may be used for Sludge's play upon spiritual ambiguity, or for David's more idealistic spiritual revelation in 'Saul'; they may be the way to Caliban's solipsistic hell, or the way to God in St John's vision of spiritual progress in 'A Death in the Desert'. Essentially, however, Browning portrays these processes as a function of character. The myth of progress is as much a fiction for St John as the presence of spirits for Sludge, and both base their claim for truth on the analogy of aesthetic illusion. But the difference lies in the psychological purpose of their vision: what for Sludge is the satisfaction of wish-fulfilment is for St John the pursuit after spiritual perfection and self-refinement in the 'type'. The potential of fiction which for Sludge turns into a bitterly frustrating irony of role-playing is for St John a source of hope and volition.

Illusion, then, is important in the process of self-realisation, and its role becomes clear when self-conception is seen as an act of pattern-making. In so far as the force of desire so frequently overrides actuality, as I have described earlier in this chapter, the monologuists in seeking self-understanding develop what may be called personal 'myths' of survival and justification. Faced with the conflicts of a multitudinous and often chaotic world, the individual finds it necessary to discover some shape or form in his experience in order to retain integrity and security. The ramifications of fiction within personality may be serious indeed in this context, where order, no matter how much a fabrication, may be crucial to the survival of a sense of individual identity. The solipsism of so many of Browning's characters is thus explained as the psychological security which results from perceiving a structured universe with the self at its centre, and in these terms Browning's monologues are more significant for their dynamics of shaping than for their portrayal of action. Indeed, because outward action in the material world is characteristically surrounded by a complex of rationalis-ations and verbal self-consciousness, physical activity tends to appear abstract in quality, as if Browning emphasises the realities of conceptualising at the expense of the realities and consequences of commitment to action. It is not action itself, then, but the pattern of action, or more correctly the conceived pattern, that is important. How action is conceived constitutes the dramatic content in Browning's poetry, where 'conceived' means both 'generated' and 'formulated'.

Although a poem such as 'Fra Lippo Lippi' portrays an energetic, dynamic personality, there is no physical action of significance within the poem itself; rather, as Lippo Lippi moves from the reported activity of his playful roguery, chasing after sportive ladies, to the proposed activity of making amends through a new religious picture, the significant action is his structuring of experience into a pattern of sin and redemption. In his eyes this plan models his behaviour in conformity with expected social patterns and he does this in order to survive, or in order to allow his private sensibility to survive. Implicit in his tone and histrionic play is a detachment from his sins, the suggestion that his acknowledged roguery is itself a pose designed to absorb and defuse public disapproval. Lippo Lippi's conception of experience, then, is one which employs the public and religious design of sin, contrition and redemption as a means of covering his impulsiveness and maintaining his need for social identity. It is a formulation which allows him to accommodate the contentions of flesh and spirit, painter and monk, individual and society.

'Andrea del Sarto' is similarly governed by patterns, by a compound of smaller fluctuations in mood and Andrea's general attempt to view his life as an arrangement of necessity. Andrea's consciousness typically shifts through an emotional version of a failing dialectic, from assertion to dissolution to stasis. Towards the end, for instance, he moves from situation to question to platitude:

> My father and my mother died of want.
> Well, had I riches of my own? you see
> How one gets rich! Let each one bear his lot.   (ll. 250–2)

From the rhetorical question which doubts his behaviour he moves to a resolution which is merely an emotional cliché, but this very retreat into passivity is a sign of Andrea's overall desire to affirm a life which could not have been otherwise, a life determined by an assigned 'lot'. With a considerable emotional investment in all that has happened, and aware that the *status quo* is all his life can be now, he must avoid the conclusion that it could have been different. 'How could it end any other way?' (l. 171) is therefore a crucial question, and it remains even as he endeavours to state his acceptance of things: 'I regret little, I would change still less./Since there my past life lies, why alter it?' (ll. 245–6). It is a question which also hovers about his fluctuations between design by providence – 'So free we seem, so fettered fast we are!' (l. 51); 'All is as God over-rules' (l. 133) – and design by choice – 'let it lie!' (l. 52); 'incentives come from the soul's self' (l. 134). His final references to Lucrezia announce that it was his choice (l. 266). Perhaps it is better that it be himself who decreed the pattern, since therein lies a sense of independence and self-respect. Another structure of necessity can be found in 'By the Fireside', where through quite a different method of representation the speaker's passivity records the way his life has been made for him by external forces. As he restructures the past during his reverie he becomes defined as the object of that past, the third person of his own recreated pattern of experience.

A pattern may not only define life but also provide it with meaning and purpose, and it is frequently those values which are implicitly sought. The speaker in 'Evelyn Hope', for example, bestows purpose on his existence through fusing the process of elegiac reconciliation with the structure of a quest for ideal love. In 'Count Gismond' also, I think the point of the speaker's account of her rescue from moral ruin is not to perpetuate a deception, but to celebrate an experience where the pattern of chivalric romance gave her life both vitality and value.[11] Without parents (l. 42) her life was in danger of losing all social status, and she was involved that eventful day in a 'play' (l. 18) which allowed her the pretence of queenship (l. 33), a role which gave her absolute value and made her the focus of admiration and envy. When this passing though pleasant fantasy was threatened by Gauthier, Count Gismond accepted the challenge, destroyed the 'lie' and transformed her pretended status into defended and therefore actualised virtue. In this her role was passive – 'I was bid/Watch Gismond for my part' (ll. 83–4) – which makes Gismond's action the focus of the performance, but it is her conception of that act which accounts for its full significance in giving her life meaning. Whether or not Gauthier's imputation was true, his confrontation threatens to destroy the whole fabric of her 'queen's-day' pageant and her response is dramatised by her in terms of a body under the 'whole strength' of torture, unable to make any reply. This inability even to reject the challenge, combined with the 'old mist' (l. 47) which hints at a too convenient blurring of her consciousness, suggests that Gauthier may have been right, but what is registered by the speaker is the pattern of simulated status, imminent destruction and redeemed honour: in Gismond she was 'quite sure that God had set/Himself to Satan' (ll. 70–1), and the end was never in doubt (ll. 81–2). She and Gismond apparently no longer refer to the event, since she changes the subject when he returns, but that need not impugn her original innocence, it may only reinforce her indulgence in reliving the triumph and excitement of an affirmed status and success. It is because Browning leaves only uncertain clues for the Countess' deception that we are left with the dominating importance of her attitude to Gismond's action. Whether she sinned or not, Gismond's God-like moral defence was an act which destroyed the 'lie' (whether hers or Gauthier's), restored her virtue, and established her social identity. For that she seems genuinely grateful and she places Gismond at the outset within a paradigm of redemption: 'Christ God who savest men, save most/Of men Count Gismond who saved me!' (ll. 1–2).

One of the most ardent expressions of the desire to perceive a design in life can be found in 'Rabbi Ben Ezra'. Here a concern with personal action has been replaced altogether by the wish for a pattern, and the speaker eventually proposes an image for existence which unites the apparent antagonism of self and world in one intermingled process of providentially controlled shaping. Action in the Rabbi's life is now what God does to him, the process of being moulded on the divine potter's wheel, and as he concludes by entreating God to 'Perfect the cup as planned!' (l. 191), he dramatises his need for a completion of the emerging form. Ben Ezra argues from the advantage of age which gains a perspective on youth, and from there he projects a perspective on life's whole. But that whole is still in God's hands and therefore the commitment to God's larger intention is an essential aspect of belief in life's shape and purpose:

> Our times are in His hand
> Who saith 'A whole I planned,
> 'Youth shows but half; trust God: see all nor be afraid!'
>
> (ll. 4–6)

Trust is indispensable, but the need is absolute – 'I must believe' (l. 30), he says of the God who provides – and the strength of that necessity increasingly emerges as one of the emotional forces underlying the Rabbi's assertions.

Psychologically, this urgency arises from the accommodation of old age and approaching death. The excitement of youth, the time when doubt was the 'spark' which meant he was more than 'brute', has now passed, and in its place he welcomes the wisdom of age which will bring truth and the peace of resolution. Yet that knowledge is still to come and his consciousness is defined by an antithesis between what has been and what is anticipated: 'Young, all lay in dispute; I shall know, being old' (l. 90). At the same time, underlying the balanced phrasing of this expression is an impetus which impels him into that future, turning his anticipation into a necessary wish. Amidst the imprisoning 'rose-mesh' of the flesh, for instance, his soul 'still yearns for rest' and 'Would' he might gain 'some prize' to match the 'Possessions of the brute' (ll. 62–6), and the intensity of this yearning emerges from the repetition of emphatic intention: 'Thence shall I pass, approved/A man. . . . And I shall thereupon/Take rest. . . . I shall try . . . And I shall weigh . . . I shall know . . .' (ll. 76–90). Superficially, he attempts to establish the certainty of logical inevitability – 'Therefore, I summon age/To grant youth's heritage' (ll. 73–4) – although the conclusion is based on moral obligation ('gifts should prove their use') and rhetorical exhortation ('Let us cry "All good things/Are ours" ') rather than logic. Similarly, he dismisses fear of death through the expectations of a moral imperative which comes from comparing age with youth: 'As it was better, youth/Should strive . . . than repose . . ./So, better, age . . . should know, than tempt/Further' (ll. 109–14). Such an argument is the effort to impose on experience a logic of obligation which will guarantee fulfilment, and in the last two stanzas that obligation is clearly assigned to God: 'since' Ben Ezra never mistook his 'end' in life, 'So' God should take His 'work' and correct its 'flaws' (ll. 183–9). From the emotional security of this logic, the concluding imperative is then addressed to God as the consummation of Ben Ezra's desire: 'Let age approve of youth, and death complete the same!' (l. 192).

The Rabbi's speech is a rather uneasy mixture of stunted phrases, balanced antitheses, clumsy constructions, fastidious qualification, exhortations, conditionals, imperatives and rhetorical questions. Yet out of this variety of tone and texture comes the sense of a struggle for order and conviction, a use of language to establish some security of purpose. The harmony of a closely rhymed stanza structure, with its two pairs of couplets and an intervening line which rhymes with the final alexandrine, often works against the contortions of sentences containing parenthetical interruptions or crude inversion to reinforce an impression of conflict underlying a tense equilibrium, the impression of a control which is wrenched from the vortex of spinning consciousness. It is an effect which is explained by the Rabbi's sense of being 'Bound dizzily' to 'the wheel of life', and by the way from amidst that 'whirl' he always pursued an end in God's purpose (ll. 183–6). The articulation of his belief is the endeavour to construct a formula which will explain his experience and aspirations; hence there emerges his conception of life as a potter's wheel and the recognition of his need for an artificer to bestow form and design:

> But I need, now as then,
> Thee, God, who mouldest men.   (ll. 181–2)

The metaphor of the potter's wheel clearly means a great deal to the Rabbi, resolving for him the many conflicts of his existence – success and failure, doubt and belief, confusion and order, body and soul, self and world, change and permanence, time and timelessness. Above all, through providing this metaphor for the unity of human experience, he assigns himself an identity in its most direct sense – sameness in all circumstances. Not only, therefore, are his outward works part of himself, but all hidden fancies and half-surmised thoughts, all instincts and uncertain purposes (ll. 139–50). This concatenation of ephemeral and multitudinous experience is given its shape and stability ('Potter and clay endure') through God's creative process. What is important for Ben Ezra is the conception of universal patterning and an understanding of God's action in relation to his own desires. The image of a divine craftsman is thus the focus of belief for a man whose life is past his own active participation, the disputatious strife of youth, and whose one aim now is passive submission to a process which will bestow form and meaningfulness: to conceive of the self as 'heaven's consummate cup' (l. 180) is to combine self-definition with spiritual value, to satisfy personal will through divine intent.

This process by which the fancies of conception may provide an image for the fulfilment of identity is more directly explained in 'A Death in the Desert', which follows 'Rabbi Ben Ezra' in *Dramatis Personae*. In order to explain his view that without the gift of conception ('man knows partly but conceives beside'; l. 582) man would lack all aspiration, hope and will to progress, St John employs an aesthetic analogy:

> 'The statuary ere he mould a shape
> 'Boasts a like gift, the shape's idea, and next
> 'The aspiration to produce the same'.   (ll. 608–10)

Through the sculptor's pursuit and indulgence of this 'falsehood', flesh may eventually be admired in what remains nevertheless 'flesh-imitating clay' (ll. 620–1). The simulated reality may be enjoyed as if the thing itself, and hence the function of illusion:

'The pattern on the Mount subsists no more,
'Seemed awhile, then returned to nothingness;
'But copies, Moses strove to make thereby,
'Serve still and are replaced as time requires:
'By these, make newest vessels, reach the type!'   (ll. 625–9)

Spiritual progress may thus be achieved through the fictions of an imitated pattern; the reality of the type is not necessary for development, since its simulation may be just as powerful a force in psychological perception. The metaphor of the potter's wheel in 'Rabbi Ben Ezra' is therefore not to be taken as a proof of providential control; it functions as an analogy which demonstrates not evidence, or even argument, but consciousness and desire, which is perhaps why it may be construed as facile optimism in the minds of those who miss its dynamic function. The image is a demonstration of a conception and of the will to an aspired end, and because it is a metaphor it acts in terms of its status as a figure of speech, as an illusion. If it were taken literally, the image would indeed be reduced to a rather simple-minded belief in divine intervention, but if perceived metaphorically (it is quite clearly called a metaphor in the poem: l. 152), it increases its effectiveness as the dramatisation of a vital conceptualising. Its meaning is not to be found in the logic or illogic of its description, but in its manifestation of a dynamic interchange between a maelstrom of external forces and a privately felt yearning for stability and purpose.

The patterns of experience in Browning's monologues emerge thus from the subjectivity of his characters, and consequently any conception of truth cannot be separated from the fictions of consciousness. Knowledge in the monologues is a function of epistemological process. This relationship can be found even in the 'Epilogue' to *Dramatis Personae*, where although the persona of the third speaker is hardly characterised as an individual in the manner of other monologuists, the subjectivity of his consciousness cannot be escaped. He points to the interaction of man and nature, and outlines an image of Arctic seas which sweep about some 'central rock', creating as they do so the illusion that the waves roam 'for its sake only' and making the rock 'The mimic monarch of the whirlpool, king/O'the current for a minute' (ll. 81–2). This image is a metaphor for the process of nature which develops the individual ego: nature dances about 'each man of us', retiring and advancing, 'As though the pageant's end were to enhance/His worth' (ll. 88–

90). Thus nature creates the illusion for each person that he is the
focus of the world's attention, and experience of nature is therefore
characterised by Browning as a pageant whose illusory reality
provides the individual with both definition and value. But this
process is similar for all men, and so the speaker perceives in it a
universal pattern which he represents as the 'one Face', presumably
of Christ, the incarnate God:

> That one Face, far from vanish, rather grows,
> Or decomposes but to recompose,
> Become my universe that feels and knows.

Like St John's 'pattern on the Mount' which continued through its
copies to represent the 'type', the imprint of Christ recurs in each
new shaping; interfused with the illusion of personal uniqueness is
the continuing design of a universal deity. At the same time, since
the face of the paradigm transforms itself into the conscious world of
the persona – his 'universe that feels and knows' – the process is
indissolubly monistic, and the identification of self and Face makes
both a conceptual idealism.

Through the detachment which results from employing a
metaphor, the speaker is able to objectify the general process
which shapes identity and forms the illusion that characterises each
ego; but at the point where that universal becomes known, where it
becomes fused with the speaker's awareness that its presence
governs him too, he must confront his own consciousness – not
Christ's universe, but 'his' universe is the knowable product of
experience. The formulations of language may propose a model –
here the metaphor of the whirlpool – and that model may be a
pattern of universal action which represents a universal truth.
However, when the model is one of the processes which shapes self-
consciousness, it is also the product of that consciousness, a fiction
about identity, and Browning acknowledges the impossibility of
detaching the conception from the process which created it when he
concludes the poem in a reversion to the speaker's subjectivity. In
this 'Epilogue' the truth of Christ is not to be found in the idea or
even in the testimony of his presence, but in his function, in the
activity of structuring consciousness through which the paradigm of
his 'Face' fulfils itself, and for Browning the reality of the paradigm
is inseparable from the illusion of an experiencing subject which
brings it into being.

Through the monologue form, Browning shows that man's conceptual patterns are essentially ambiguous in what they represent. Any conception of experience is a product of consciousness so that in it world and self are intertwined in an unconscious fiction of identity. This is the ironic result of the Romantic desire to achieve self-knowledge through self-projection; it is the reason why the monologues so often draw attention to the subjective sources of a dramatised image, and it is why they so often incorporate an ambiguous relationship between reference to an outward universality and the reflexiveness of an inner self-generation. Through portraying the tendency of men and women to equate the pattern of their perception with the structure of their world, and through portraying the use of illusion in human subjectivity, Browning plays upon the central ambiguity in *Pippa Passes*: whether a pattern of coincidence is the sign of a providential plan or simply of man's need to believe in one. The monologue form seems continually to imply such a question, and while the ironies in a speaker's argument may indicate the discrepancy between two directions of metaphoric meaning, what that discrepancy really suggests about the process of human thought is an interweaving of perception and conception, an interfusion of fact and fancy which shapes meaning (value and purpose) as a function of individual identity.

5 Histrionic Action in *The Ring and the Book*

The histrionic action in psychological experience which recurs in Browning's monologues means that the qualities of aesthetic illusion in his poetry do not merely provide an analogy or model for life, but are also characteristic of its nature. Browning consequently has shifted the focus for the drama metaphor that 'all the world's a stage' from external behaviour into internal psychological action. Nowhere is this more clear than in *The Ring and the Book* where we are confronted with an image of society based on the juxtaposed subjectivities of its members rather than a series of interrelated events which merge into a unified whole. Such a shift represents a seriously altered view of human experience. Whereas the image of the world as stage tends to emphasise the individual's part in some larger plot, his action as a contribution to some externally conceived design, in *The Ring and the Book* the unifying story of external events is made so obvious as to be virtually superfluous, and what is emphasised is the individual's powers of conception, his ability to retell the story according to need and predilection. Instead of the individual becoming absorbed into the dramatic plan of some larger incident, the incident is absorbed into the individual's structure of explanation. This process begins with the poet's own several versions in book one and continues with the ensuing speakers to make the main effect of reading through the monologues not so much an emerging truth about one event as the multiple transformations of the event when it is sifted through human consciousness. Browning's mimetic method, which imitates not the world but men thinking about the world, is thus taken to its logical conclusion in the form of *The Ring and the Book*, and in this achievement the poem is a major aesthetic statement of nineteenth-century subjectivism.

For Browning, the mind as well as the world is a stage, and that is not to say he separates the two arenas. His focus on the way consciousness isolates the self from others does not deny the

individual as a participant in social action. Any implicit dualism of
self and body or perception and performance is an irony of
consciousness rather than a reality of experience, and his characters
are all participants as well as onlookers, actors on the public stage as
well as the private. Indeed their speeches are made in relationship
to a trial, a clearly defined social forum for the justification and
judgement of public action. However, in this trial the truth of action
is rarely in question and the focus is on interpretation, not
judgement, as Guido and Caponsacchi both indicate. Guido does
this when admitting he committed the murders – 'There's the
irregular deed: you want no more / Than right interpretation of the
same' (v.113–14) – and Caponsacchi when beginning his address –
'let me . . . interpret you / The mystery of this murder' (vi.72–4).[1]
Therefore, while the poem places characters within a defined social
context, portraying the interweaving of society and its members, the
radical structure of juxtaposed monologues means that the emphasis remains on individual drama, on the way each self, through
acting as the subject of its own perception, conceives of all
experience as if its own. Each monologue may be read as a mode of
understanding whose meaning, following Browning's practice in
Men and Women and *Dramatis Personae*, is a function of consciousness
and its concomitant, language: 'how else know we save by worth of
word?' (1.837).

Since in this particular method of formalising collective subjectivity all interaction between characters becomes a reported act,
part of one character's recollected or hypothesised version, it may
seem that intersubjectivity is not an issue and that *The Ring and the
Book* is set apart from the general trend of subjectivism as it appears
in other Victorian works. J. Hillis Miller, for example, has pointed
out that the novel is characteristically 'a structure of interpenetrat-
ing minds' and that in most nineteenth-century novels 'the
characters are aware of themselves in terms of their relations to
others', seeking to fulfil themselves 'by way of other people'.[2]
Certainly Browning portrays the self-consciousness, the awareness
of a self separate from others, which is different from the main means
of self-identification in novels of the period, but through this
Browning does not disavow the importance of intersubjective
experience: he dramatises its ironies. A clue to the point is provided
by Professor Miller's observance of a relationship between
Victorian novels and the dramatic monologue. He suggests that the
Victorian novel, which is often based on the 'indirect discourse' of a

narrator, is a version of a monologue 'in which the monologuist superimposes his own voice, judgement, and mind on those of the character' (p. 3), and this mode of fiction, an extension of the Romantic role-playing phenomenon of sympathetic identification, is made possible by 'the fact that one can in language imagine oneself as having direct access to another mind' (p. 3). Miller thus views Browning's monologues as embryonic novels, but *The Ring and the Book* is more than an embryo of this sort and just as complex in its development of intersubjectivity as any comparable novel. Indeed in Miller's sense of the narrator as monologuist, each book in the poem is a form of novel, a construction where each character in turn relates a sequence of events and discusses other people in such a way as to superimpose on all his mind and judgement. Browning evolves a series of novel-like narratives and a whole web of interrelationships: characters among themselves, protagonists with onlookers and observers with their neighbours, between author and speaker, author and reader, reader and character. Underlying all this, however, is Browning's method of presentation which makes the interpenetration of minds dependent on the conceptions of a separate mind. The experience of intersubjectivity in this method is a relationship therefore not between two minds, but between one mind and its conception of another, and it is a relationship based on an interaction between fictions, between the conceptualising of self and of the other. The experience of this process is clearly itself a reality. To the speakers their fancy is a fact, and the 'fact' that language allows them to imagine 'direct access to another mind' reinforces the assumption of a substantive truth in what they perceive. For the reader, however, such assumptions are always potentially ironic: the power of sympathetic imagination may be restricted by the power of an interfering ego, so that experience and truth do not necessarily coincide. Also, while the reader is in the privileged position of an omniscient observer, and the speakers' reports may overlap within his reading of the poem, such an effect is still dependent on the extrapolations of *his* separate mind, since it is he who must compare one reported conversation with another, interpret the interpretations. Because of the form of the poem, intersubjective experience is presented within the natural conditions of irony – juxtaposition and not interpenetration. *The Ring and the Book* therefore enforces the irony that any model which objectifies human experience is itself subject to the reflexiveness of subjectivity, whether of maker or observer.

To imagine access to other minds is to dramatise others as well as the self, and that is a form of imitation where, in passages which purport to represent what was thought or said, a speaker pretends for a moment to be someone else. Since all speakers engage in this means of reproducing others, they are alike in repeating various acts of mimicry; furthermore, they all reflect the poet whose own continuing mimicry animates the whole poem, and he in turn imitates God, who is the original creator of all heaven and earth. Each speaker is therefore an imitation poet and histrionic action thus pervades the poem as a repetitive image of 'Mimic creation' (1.740). In an extended passage in book one, the poet explains that man can only repeat God's process in 'due degree', not creating but resuscitating life (1.707–72). Because 'man makes not man', the poet is instead a magician who raises ghosts, investing his energies in a 'galvanism for life', a simulation of experience which allows the dead 'to live again'. Through this imitation of creativity the poet provides characters with the illusion of continuing existence, and in their own way or 'degree' they repeat the process, since the demands of the trial, with its accompanying rumours and speculation, require a continuing revival of the past, a repeated resuscitation of event and attitude. The monologues are in effect a parade of feigning, ghosts conjuring up phantoms and phantoms engaged in an ever-receding process of mimic action. Consequently, from the opening image in book one, the ring which copies 'Etrurian circlets' and was shaped 'By Castellani's imitative craft' (1.1–4), reality is displayed as a simulation, as not the thing itself. For Pompilia, for instance, 'Marriage on earth seems such a counterfeit, / Mere imitation of the inimitable' (VII.1824–5), and if that is a paradox which is coloured by the doom of impossibility, it is explained by her idealising the angels who become married without marrying, by her desire to forsake the flesh and seek an androgynous fulfilment which would achieve union without division (VII.1827–37). Apparently she does not realise the irony that what she proposes is but another imitation, to 'Be as the angels'.

Perhaps the most extreme example of histrionic simulation is the second lawyer's monologue. It is quite directly a mimic act, what Bottinius *would* say if he could speak at the trial instead of merely handing in a written submission, and he affirms totally the view that explanations matter more than fact, taking up the hypothesis that Guido's version of events might be correct, in order to explain it in Pompilia's favour. He simultaneously denies that what Guido says is true and so facts are of no consequence: he defends a fiction, which is sufficient.

> Thus
> Would I defend the step,–were the thing true
> Which is a fable.   (ix.637–9)

He justifies this approach through an analysis of subjective transformation in his opening analogy of the painter. Life's realities provide models for the artist whose 'brain' then changes them into the 'soul' of his picture (ix.86–101); mere copies or transcripts from life are 'fact and false', whereas the subjective transfiguring of matter, 'a spirit-birth conceived of flesh', is 'Truth rare and real' (ix.106–7). This is the irony of Romantic subjectivism applied to legal enquiry, and given this awareness of the artifice in human perception, it then naturally follows that Bottinius discerns in Pompilia, in terms of her performance in Guido's story, a magnificent feigning. He explains that through the need for survival:

> licit end
> Enough was found in mere escape from death,
> To legalize our means illicit else
> Of feigned love, false allurement, fancied fact.
>
> (ix.525–8)

Her life is thus conceived by him as a series of admirable poses: 'O splendidly mendacious!' (ix.838), he expostulates about her claim that she could not read or write. Through this attitude, however, his speech becomes nothing less than an effort to dispense altogether with defining reality, for if he can explain successfully the most damaging fiction about Pompilia then facts are unnecessary.

It may seem that the dispersal of reality through levels of simulation is contradicted by the strong sense of physical tangibility which emerges from the poem's richness of detail and imagery. But Browning does not deny the literalness of the material and social milieu, nor the force with which physical sensation may impinge on the mind; he simply focuses attention on the interfusion of mind with that sensation, on the way language allows characters to invent meaning, just as Bottinius' painter dispenses with the factualness of 'studies' and transforms them in 'the inner spectrum' of his mind.

The images and metaphors of language are themselves but a mimic reality and the knowledge which comes with consciousness is consequently rooted in similitude, although as always the illusion is itself a reality. The image of a reflection has its own existence and may even suggest a truth through exposing a flaw in what it reflects, like Judas' 'mimic dream' which urged the virtues of not dreaming: 'That to keep wide awake is man's best dream' (IX.1088–1108). Therefore, while conceiving of self and others in a retrospective narration is to assign them all roles in a fiction and to diffuse original acts through several imitations, this histrionic endeavour is for these very reasons a representation of reality, a realisation of Browning's insight into the conceptualising which informs all perception and constitutes all identity.

Through adding the ironies of intersubjectivity to the histrionic acts of individual minds, Browning takes the problems of identity further in *The Ring and the Book* than is possible in most single monologues, allowing the reader to observe how characters shape events in their own narrative, and also how they mould each other, how individuals become identified through the way they are absorbed into other people's simulations as well as through the role they are assigned in their own. Personality as well as reality is thus potentially diffuse: from the self as self-defined to the self as its many versions conceived in the minds of others. Such a possibility has particular consequences for Guido, for example, who attempts to exonerate himself by dispersing his identity among several roles, selves for whose action he may deny responsibility. At the same time, if the substance and singleness of self becomes dispersed among its versions, it is also, like the interpretation of behaviour and guilt, a subject for redefinition and recreation. In so far as resuscitation of the past involves the dramatising of an imitation self, a review of identity is almost inevitable, and while the act of self-mirroring which is involved generally leads to the reinforcement of stasis, in at least one case it suggests the possibilities for change and growth.

Of all the speakers, Guido and Caponsacchi probably provide the two richest examples of histrionic action in character: Guido who wants to hide in a plethora of roles and Caponsacchi who seeks an authentic identity but who is tormented by his sense of failure. In his first monologue Guido defines himself through his social role, claiming like Mr Sludge that he merely performed what others expected of him, and accepting the fate which made him the eldest son of an aristocratic family:

> Will my lords, in the plenitude of their light,
> Weigh well that all this trouble has come on me
> Through my persistent treading in the paths
> Where I was trained to go, – wearing that yoke
> My shoulder was predestined to receive,
> Born to the hereditary stoop and crease?   (v.122–7)

With his personality defined by training and position, he dramatises himself as a fish which was 'stranded' when the means to fulfil that identity were lacking. Through flaunting this image of a noble potential which became ruined by an alien environment (v.176–81), he prepares for his main thrust in this monologue of representing himself as a man whose rightful identity was predetermined by birth and yet unfulfilled because of circumstances. Tied to the duties of eldest son and therefore denied the alternative roles of soldier or priest, he attempts to minimise the signs of his own volition and portray himself as acquiescent and willing to do whatever his role requires of him. Consequently his attack on Pompilia rests largely on his complaint that she refused to play her part in the marriage pact while he played his (v.607–10). He focuses attention therefore on the individual as social performer and hence perceives Pompilia's individuality as an abstract principle – 'With a wife I look to find all wifeliness' (v.604) – and her humanity as the mere functionalism of role-fulfilment: 'Pompilia's duty was – submit herself, / Afford me pleasure, perhaps cure my bile' (v.718–19).

The irony is that this investment of identity in a system of social determinism removes his own individuality in much the same way. The point of the exercise is that he may claim implicit freedom from responsibility because actions were not determined by him, but the corollary is that his formulation of a dutiful self which subordinates private will to public expectation ironically undermines the very unity of that self, through dispersing its control among a multiplicity of forces – family, friends, church and law. His responses to these influences then tend to reduce his personality to the level of conflicting rationalisations that begin to cancel each other out. The potential for this trend is revealed by Guido himself when he points to the inconsistency of views about the Castelnuovo incident (v.1068–86), but the point is more clearly seen in his account of the murder itself. There he claims that he acted from unconscious, unseeing impulsiveness:

> how I was mad,
> Blind, stamped on all, the earth-worms with the asp,
> And ended so.   (v.1667–9)

And also that he performed God's will: 'I did / God's bidding and man's duty, so, breathe free' (v.1702–3). Both explanations are in accord with his character as a pawn for other forces, but they contradict each other, since an act of irrational, undiscriminating violence is at odds with the claim of having a defined moral purpose. On the other hand Guido need not be consistent so long as he is not responsible. The shifting among masters may render his identity diffuse, but in his eyes that need not make him culpable, and his moral challenge is a challenge also to assumptions about personality. As one of Browning's most histrionic characters he is one of the most ambiguous. Through demonstrating the conviction with which roles may be simulated and through focusing on the performance of a socially defined identity, this monologue implicitly questions the very existence of personality as an independent, unified force. Guido can be said to exist, as in his second monologue, only as a self-dramatising consciousness, defending himself through transferring responsibility from himself as puppet to social determinism as puppet-master. If this view makes him a victim of society's conflicting requirements, then that is his point.

Caponsacchi's personality is also moulded by other forces, but through the self-consciousness which his monologue generates he is able to develop a detachment from that social definition. In this speech he needs to redeem an action and an identity which, having just learnt of Guido's fatal attack on Pompilia, he now knows to be failures. Consequently, his monologue is the record of a complex and tormented consciousness as it wrestles with the discrepancy between what he would have done (destroyed Guido and saved Pompilia) and what was actually achieved (an 'ineffective help' which merely hastened Pompilia's death). Through the opportunities for reviewing his experience which are provided by the mimic actions of retrospection, he recaptures the move away from his identity as a social puppet, and through this same process discovers a self-determining voice of personal desire. While as he says, in terms of the world as a stage, his 'part / Is done' (vi.167–8), that part is

now re-enacted for the stage of the court and his own mind, where
its significance is internalised, reviewed and finally transfigured.

That Caponsacchi is a 'puppet' of both heaven and earth is first
indicated in the poet's introduction (1.1019–22). That his early
identity as priest was nurtured by his family and then redefined by
his Bishop is clear from his own account (VI.240–335). He is assigned
the ambivalent role of Church troubador, which is designed not to
renounce the world, but to sustain it, bringing it to the Church, and
he is taught the politics of success, subtleties of influence and the arts
of social illusion: '"A polished presence, a genteel manner, wit/At
will, and tact at every pore"' (VI.371–2). Thus he passively serves
the Church, employing his skills to meet expectations. What is not
quite so obvious perhaps is that he is also a puppet of his masculinity,
and that in his response to Pompilia he does not initiate the grand
action of a self-determining hero so much as replace one mistress
with another. Just as his Bishop supplies the rationalisation and
pattern for his role as priest, so it is Pompilia who finally provides the
initiative and impetus for his rescue by evoking his sense of manly
virtue and suggesting another pattern to fulfil. Caponsacchi is
gripped by the power of an image, by the force of his own
conception which internalises Pompilia as the abstraction of her
'beautiful sad strange smile' (VI.399, 412, 436), and at his first
meeting with her he sees her as an icon, at 412, as the 'framed' image of a
Madonna, an object of potential worship (VI.701–7). Such a
conception places himself in the subordinate role – he is only
prevented from kneeling by her sudden disappearance – and prepares for the demands of her speech, when she announces her need
for 'good true love' and says she has been told he would die for her
(VI.861). Through her address Pompilia imposes upon him the role
which ironically was outlined by Guido (' "you that proffer help" ',
VI.788), and she provides him with a self-conception which in the
context of his growing desire for an honest belief he would hardly
want to deny: ' "you are true, have been true, will be true" '
(VI.878). Even in recounting this miracle of her presence Caponsacchi indicates that the initiative was hers: 'Pompilia spoke, and I at
once received . . . she chose / To summon me and signify her
choice' (VI.918–21). Certainly his acceptance of this new possibility
leads to a turmoil of excitement and an ecstatic transformation:
'Into another state, under new rule / I knew myself was passing swift
and sure' (VI.964–5). Yet his expression shows that in this new state
he is still under rule, passively submitting to 'the invasion' which

brought 'new things' (VI.947–8) and lying in wait for 'the proper throe' (VI.972). He may have discovered in this submission to the determinism of experience a new authenticity of self-sacrifice, but at the same time it leads to a confusion of authorities, a conflict between the demands of human passion and the commitment to spiritual duty. Man or priest, each is a puppet, and each is pulled by conflicting strings. His rationalisation that ' "Duty to God is duty to her" ' (VI.1030) will not do, for instance, since any service which means inaction is clearly not a service to Pompilia.

It is a curious feature of Caponsacchi's narrative that despite the many suggestions of an impulsive emotionalism, only once does he really act spontaneously. That is when finally after long delay he arranges the flight from Arezzo, and even that action is essentially reaction, due less to his own volition than to his shame at Pompilia's assertiveness as she perceives in him a singleness of purpose that he could not discover for himself:

'You are again here, in the self-same mind,
I see here, steadfast in the face of you, –
You grudge to do no one thing that I ask.
Why then is nothing done? You know my need.' (VI.1068–71)

He does indeed act, but it is hardly the immediate seizing of intuitive truth which he would like to believe in retrospect. He is too much embedded in consciousness to be a man of unthinking action, and in his retrospective reflection there is a consistent interplay between pride in his efforts to save Pompilia and a terrible frustration at having to acknowledge his weakness. He tried to master the destiny of events – ' "Now follow me as I were fate!" ' (VI.1076) – but too often simply found himself powerless: 'I could not choose' (VI.1417). The most intensive moment for chagrin is at Castelnuovo when although it was Caponsacchi who dressed as the cavalier, as ' "the lover in the smart disguise / With the sword" ' (VI.1465–6), it was Pompilia who actually performed the cavalier's action by leaping at her husband with sword in hand. In dismissing his religious duties when he left Arezzo (VI.1118–23) and in speculating about what he might say to a certain bishop (VI.1260–5), Caponsacchi seems to have thought he was rejecting the servant priest and activating the masterful man. But Pompilia suggests otherwise, that he had swapped one position of servitude for another:

'Who was it –
What woman were you used to serve this way,
Be kind to, till I called you and you came?'   (VI.1231–3)

He was hurt by this question ('I did not like that word') and by her continuing to see him in the role of priest (VI.1269–74), and while he may have attempted an act of self-sacrifice, a transforming of priest into cavalier and courtly lover, the effort redeemed neither Pompilia nor himself. As he later suggests, there was certainly a princess and a dragon, and there 'should have been a Saint George also' (VI.1775–7), but there was not. His role as knight-errant fails and it is openly relinquished at Castelnuovo when he chooses the Church and Rome for judgement as 'priest' instead of the Duke as 'Tuscan noble' (VI.1582–4).

However, if Caponsacchi does not master his destiny in the escape from Arezzo, he does move in the act of this monologue itself towards an assertion of feelings which are not governed by social expectation. His histrionic method, like Guido's, is a means of detaching himself from his earlier performances and from the definitions which other people make for him. Whereas for Guido this process meant a deliberate dispersing of identity among its fragmented versions, for Caponsacchi it leads to the realisation of an authentic independence. Through relating his puppet-like roles as priest and lover, he objectifies and so distances his own passivity, and in acknowledging his failure to save Pompilia he separates himself from the hero figure of St George, of whom he was but a pale imitation. What Caponsacchi discovers is a self which may dispense with all preconceived roles, and it emerges finally through his passion and frustration when he cancels his role as witness ('I have done with being judged'), defies the court's capacity for misinterpretation ('in contempt / For all misapprehending ignorance / O' the human heart') and invites the judges to defrock him ('Unpriest me, rend the rags o' the vestment, do'). This passage (VI.1860–73) is a climactic gesture which relinquishes all artifice, including the trappings of the priest, and flaunts the self as a passionate being which stands alone on the basis of known experience – that he 'was blessed / By the revelation of Pompilia'. It is a histrionic gesture in its grand flamboyance:

There!
Such is the final fact I fling you, Sirs,
To mouth and mumble and misinterpret: there!
'The priest's in love', have it the vulgar way!

Yet, paradoxically, it is this very histrionic extravagance which achieves his separation from the garb of priestly humility and judicious explanation. This is not the logic of evidence but the affirmation of identity, a realisation and acknowledgement of the changed self-awareness which Pompilia has brought him – her 'revelation'. The redemption of the past therefore occurs precisely in its transformation, through Caponsacchi's dramatising of a passion which explains the universe, making Pompilia a saint worthy of worship and Guido the counterpart of Judas, a betrayer of all that is good (VI.1881–1954). In this way Caponsacchi shapes the past into a fiction which gives meaning to his experience: it is a fiction because the impulse which brought the 'spark of truth' from their souls was not as pure in its original manifestation as in retrospect it seems (VI.1812–21), and yet it is a truth because significance is indeed the product of consciousness in this context. It is a fiction of identity which arises from an authenticity of passion.

Still, neither does Caponsacchi identify absolutely with Pompilia's revelation. Despite their strength and reality, the feelings of his love for Pompilia and hate for Guido no longer dominate his mind as they did earlier and his consciousness detaches itself from them also. His desire that Guido should be allowed to die in an agony of rejection and loneliness is a dramatisation of his frustrations and chagrin in failing to deal with Guido himself, but the objectification of his feelings which occurs in that act leads to the self-consciousness of a mock-amazement at his digression:

> Why, Sirs, what's this? Why, this is sorry and strange!
> Futility, divagation: this from me
> Bound to be rational, justify an act
> Of sober man!   (VI.1955–8)

This is a mixture of dismay and irony, of the fear of harming Pompilia again and an awareness of the irony if he did so – 'A pretty sarcasm for the world!' (VI.1960). While separating self from priest and self from passion, he thus remains conscious also of the court's requirements and of the need for a more reasoned explanation of his behaviour. His is a complex consciousness and he moves less towards a resolution of personality than towards an accommodation of its facets. If the histrionics of imagination allow a freedom which enables him to reject the superficiality of modish religion and seek an honest self-understanding, then at the same time he must recognise that the fulfilment of certain potential is 'but play with an imagined life' (VI.2081). His desire to live with Pompilia in marriage is 'Mere delectation, meet for a minute's dream!' (VI.2097). His claim that he withdraws from this fiction of possibility feeling 'content' (VI.2104) is no doubt the reimposition of a necessary reality, but the loss of that possibility nevertheless hurts: 'O great, just, good God! Miserable me!' In this final, terrible antithesis, therefore, his awe for God's providence exists beside a despairing sense of the cost to himself. Man and priest remain in uneasy juxtaposition, though they are encompassed by a consciousness which through dramatising all aspects realises and knows them. Caponsacchi does not achieve an identity which fuses and fulfils all desires, but he formulates an understanding which is redemptive despite its painfulness. Pompilia was a 'revelation' in so far as she revealed to him his inner life. From the moment when his mind first internalised her image, becoming caught in its power, she led him to a strength of feeling which he could discover and acknowledge as his own, and thence to an assertion of independence in court, an affirmation of self which he had not achieved before. In the act of the monologue, then, the dynamics of self-consciousness and the histrionic action through which they function lead Caponsacchi to an expression of authentic self-awareness, separate from role definition or imposed expectation.

If Caponsacchi finally stands alone with his desire, so too does Guido in his second monologue. However, whereas Caponsacchi's histrionic capacity enables him to accommodate contending factions, Guido discovers no similar means of attaining authenticity, no equivalent self-knowledge. He may affirm his existence through an image of natural villainy, but he cannot see himself from any other perspective than one which justifies his destructiveness or defines what he has been. Whereas Caponsacchi imagines the possibility of difference and grows through a changing consciousness, Guido contemplates only sameness and the continuity of sameness: on earth, until death, 'All that was, is; and must forever be' (XI.2399). Even in heaven there will be 'something changeless' at the heart of him, allowing him to know himself (XI.2394–5), and the only future fulfilment he proposes is an Ovidian metamorphosis which would enhance and glut his existing 'wolf-nature' (XI.2060). This sense of stasis or marked lack of development emerges from Guido's idea of himself as a made personality; he admits he is a mistake, but that is not his fault, he claims, who did not make himself (XI.939–40). The creation of identity is therefore an irrelevancy to Guido, which makes one suggestion about Guido's role-playing beside the point: 'for Guido there can hardly be a personality to create or discover since he is committed to the principles of disorientation and destruction'.[3] Guido is not 'committed' to anything; he simply acts in accord with his own nature, or so he conceives of himself in this monologue. Similarly, he does not 'choose' evil: 'for Browning the choice of evil is a rejection of natural order which can only result in the destruction of self'.[4] Rather, Browning suggests that it is lack of choice and acceptance of naturalness which may lead to self-destruction, since Guido's kind of responsiveness is as natural to him as is Caponsacchi's to Caponsacchi; and it would have been better, as Guido himself points out, if he *had* been made to choose, 'indulge / Or else renounce my instincts' (xi.820–1), instead of being encouraged by the clergy to equivocate, to cover his 'wolf's-skin' with 'sheep's wool' (xi.824–5). In Guido's second monologue, Browning dramatises a man who when cornered by the world rejects its authority, constructing for himself whatever images will defend his self-respect. Whereas in his first speech Guido dramatised himself as a social man, conforming to the demands of social opinion, now when finding himself judged by society and religion, he represents himself as the natural man, acting only from instinct, without artificial constraint, and challenging conventional morality by refusing to accept its assumptions.

Guido continues, therefore, to portray himself as a victim of circumstances, now shifting responsibility from society to destiny: all is 'fate not fortune' (xi.1733). He conceives of himself as the victim of a plot, betrayed by his friends, whether the clergy or his fellow murderers, and his mimicry of others is generally governed by an all-embracing cynicism. He mocks the cardinals' demands for repentance, for instance, by implying they merely seek exoneration for their part in his death:

> I ought to raise my ruined head, allege
> Not simply I pushed worse blade o' the pair,
> But my antagonist dispensed with steel!   (xi.491–3)

And he parodies public reaction to the Comparini:

> Inconscious agents they, the silly-sooth,
> Of heaven's retributive justice on the strong
> Proud cunning violent oppressor – me!   (xi.1230–2)

Through representing the folly and hypocrisy in others in this way, Guido reinforces his sense of injustice, and his capacity for parody and for spinning elaborate hypotheses, such as outlining the story he would have told if Pompilia had died immediately (XI.1704–24), is for him a conservative attribute. By dramatising other perspectives he confirms his own; he uses fictions not to discover a new self, but to reinforce the old.

Essentially he will do or say anything to survive: 'One must try each expedient to save life' (XI.852). The histrionic action in this monologue consequently consists of Guido's efforts to insert a linguistic screen between himself and the guillotine. Aware of its imminence, he struggles with an implicit paradox of consciousness: while 'each minute's talk / Helps push [the machine] an inch the nearer' (XI.847–8), talking also removes its immediacy, prolonging the illusion of continuing existence. That he indulges in mere rhetoric, he acknowledges: 'All's but a flourish, figure of rhetoric!' (XI.351), 'My fight is figurative, blows i' the air' (XI.2320), 'All was folly – I laughed and mocked!' (XI.2419). But his hypotheses serve a psychological purpose, for identity in this context is whatever fiction he can persuasively flaunt as a viable past, a past which will protect him, perhaps even save him, from the threat of extinction. Tied to past actions, he cannot deny what literally occurred, but he can place events within a framework of explanation which makes them the plausible product of naturalness and instinct – 'Why should you master natural caprice?' (XI.1439). He may even suggest a hero's death for himself, since in the warfare between his hate and the world he provides the 'spectacle / Of a brave fighter who succumbs to odds / That turn defeat to victory' (XI.1801–3). Yet the images of his self-description, however spontaneously frank they seem, are always dramatisations which provide only the illusion of self-analysis. The whole suggestion, for instance, that his feelings and actions towards Pompilia were the product of an amoral naturalness develops not from conviction but from overt speculation: 'Say that I hated her for no one cause / Beyond my pleasure so to do, – what then?' (XI.1434–5). Similarly, the notorious wolf-image is not a description he wilfully seeks for himself, but is bestowed on him by the Pope: Guido says he is 'the shuddering sheep', whom the Pope 'calls a wolf' (XI.405). It becomes a useful metaphor, which Guido acknowledges as such – 'How that staunch image serves at every turn!' (XI.1179) – and it illustrates for him a suitable fusion of natural feeling and self-serving ferocity, the 'proper instinct of defence' (XI.2303). But despite his flaunting of the image as if himself, he maintains a detachment from it, an awareness that it is a figurative expression and therefore a hypothesis: 'That's the wolf-nature. Don't mistake my trope!' (XI.2318). Even the staunch refusal to admit moral fault which he implicitly uses to identify his pagan pragmatism becomes a mere ploy when he reveals that he expected his confessors not to 'slay' an impenitent soul (XI.2231–3). Guido, therefore, whatever the degree of identification he may exercise towards passing images, always retains a separate consciousness. Such a separation is explicit when he claims that he has learnt from experience – 'I'm practised, grown fit guide for Guido's self' (XI.1462) – and in the distinction between 'self' and 'I' lies the separation between self as subject and self as object which Guido uses to avoid the pain and shock of full self-knowledge.

In this self-protection the difference from Caponsacchi is apparent. When Caponsacchi describes his dream of life with Pompilia as a fancy, 'Mere delectation', he exercises a self-knowledge which proffers the potential fulfilment while recognising both its impossibility and his own desire; it is a recognition of several realities, a self-consciousness which asserts the fiction while knowing it to be such. Guido also observes the fictive dimension of his 'tropes', but the self-consciousness which is a release into self-realisation for Caponsacchi remains a limitation of perspective for Guido. He is too eager to assert passing identification with images which remain only possibilities. At the conclusion of his monologue, for example, he identifies himself with the independent strength of a 'strong tree' and with the Athenian who died drinking bull's blood, 'fit for men like me' (XI.2407–11); but in that phrase is the self-justifying illusion of value, or fiction of identity, which is shown immediately to be false. It is Guido's imagination and power of self-projection which is finally and ironically the source of his restricted growth. His ability to portray himself as a man of nature means he remains the puppet of his instincts and a self whose existence is bound by physical being. Death is therefore intolerable despite his hypothesis about a future life; that is a meaningless speculation because only one more dramatised possibility which he does not really believe in. The power of Guido's histrionic consciousness, in its evasion of responsibility for his detached selves, becomes consequently a trap which leads to panic and disintegration when consciousness itself must end. Without an acted image he has no individual definition. He is an actor therefore who is nothing without a role, and when threatened with extinction the histrionic man collapses into stricken histrionics, clinging desperately to the role of victim in one last plea: 'Pompilia, will you let them murder me?' Guido *is* a victim: the ironic victim of his consciousness, of his paradoxical but very natural ability to conceive of self without self-understanding.[5]

The differences between Caponsacchi and Guido suggest the varying possibilities for the histrionic acts of self-conception; they may be a means of growth or simply a prison of psychological stasis, or as in the case of Pompilia they may produce the irony of a denial of experience which at the same time characterises experience. All that seemed most real to Pompilia dissolved into a series of fictions – her parents who were not her parents, her husband who denied her, and her child who 'withdraws into a dream/As the rest do' (VII.213–14). She perceives her experience therefore as the fabric of a dream (VII.584–606), a process which enables her to handle the pain of her existence by denying its substance. She may not adapt to the world's realities, but she is able through this device of consciousness to accommodate both experience and conception, and thereby sustain belief in her integrity:

> I am held up, amid the nothingness,
> By one or two truths only – thence I hang,
> And there I live, – the rest is death or dream,
> All but those points of my support.   (VII.603–6)

The 'truths' which support Pompilia, her 'prayer to God', her 'hope' and her 'fancy', are the intangible realities of feeling and need. Yet hope turns into the 'hand' of her friend and the fancy becomes her 'child'; therefore these feelings, reinforced by the physical presences which they become for her, remain as personal verities while other equally real impressions of experience fade into the 'nothingness' which characterises all else. Psychological processes such as this, most of which like Pompilia's are born from some necessary illusion ('"Life means with me successful feigning death"'; VII.1004), account for the general displacement of reality in the poem. As I have suggested, with Browning's focus on the way experience is filtered through individual minds, reality shifts from a predetermining subject of experience to become an object of subjective perception. The literal fact is absorbed into systems of explanation and consequently all understanding rests on epistemological ambiguity. Distinctions between fancy and fact are blurred amidst simulated behaviour and imitated action, and the multiplication of narrators, far from making things more certain, simply increases the fanciful quality of the 'real'.

However, this is not to say that such a mélange turns the poem into a relativist's paradise, for even though meaning is what speakers make it, one more transformation among a series, irony functions as usual in Browning's work to reveal each character's role as subject and therefore the limits to his perspective. In this sense, for instance, Guido is not even right for himself on his own terms, for unless it is argued that he exercises an unconscious desire to sabotage himself, he establishes no secure or independent identity despite his claims to boldness (XI.2413). His view of man remains cynical and diminished because he can see no more than a pervasive duplicity in human action from which he cannot exempt himself, tainting himself thereby through his conception of others. It is the reflexiveness of conceptualising which is always the ironic trap. Yet, the ironies of self-knowledge apart, Guido is at the same time clearly justified in taking this view: men are indeed hypocrites and human action is indeed dogged by deception, as Guido's whole experience with his family, the Church, and the Comparini has demonstrated. Or so it has seemed to Guido, and his formulation of experience in book eleven not only represents the way he has grasped the real, but for him constitutes the real. Therefore the ironic undercutting of monologues is not by itself sufficient to deny that the poem portrays a relativist philosophy, and the technique of juxtaposing separate speakers continually encourages a consideration of one monologue 'relative' to another. Relativity, however, would have no absolute point of reference, and in *The Ring and the Book* there is a predetermined and clearly enunciated authorial attitude which establishes such a standard for measuring moral behaviour and which functions through the obvious assignment of archetypal roles. These images have been often observed by critics and are largely taken from the Christian patterns of sin and redemption, God and Satan, Adam and Eve and the serpent in Eden, and from the mythic pattern of Perseus and Andromeda with its Christian analogue of St George and the Dragon.[6] Although the roles may be variously applied by different speakers, they nevertheless form a continuing cluster of moral associations and a framework therefore for moral interpretation, whether by author or character.

It is worth noting, though, that the poet's outline of the

Franceschini murder in book one is not a prophecy of things to come, but an account of events which have already occurred. The reader, then, is not confronted with a providential plan which is about to be fulfilled as a demonstration of divine or authorial purpose, but with a sequence of incidents which is fixed because viewed in retrospect. Since the poet does not create the story but simply resuscitates it, his mimic creation anticipates and encompasses similar acts by the speakers who follow. Like them he is engaged in a retrospective reconstruction of the past, and he too may interpret what happened or colour its impact by altering his principle of selection. For example, the version which overtly mixes his fancy with fact (1.679) and portrays events as the grand action of St George and the devil is made so excessive in language and tone as to be at the same time a self-parody. It is therefore an admitted melodrama, a conception which acknowledges the way it replaces common realism with common exaggeration. In the very telling this cosmic battle of good and evil is both asserted and parodied, so that it too is inseparable from its making, from the consciousness which is manifested in that peculiarly ironic mixture of dramatic gesture and self-awareness, enthusiasm and mockery, which flaunts the grandeur of the moral conflict while admitting its comic absurdity.[7] Any idealising or moral patterning thus emerges from the linguistic play which shapes meaning and understanding.

In the monologues themselves, as speakers elaborate details of the original events, the incredible disparity of feeling during those events, and a general uncertainty and conflict of purpose, become apparent. Pompilia is puzzled by the reasons for her crumbling world; Caponsacchi's aims were mixed and ill-defined when he arranged the escape; Guido knows but hardly understands his hatred; Half-Rome, Other Half-Rome and Tertium Quid confuse motives in the murder story with their own desires and impulses; the two lawyers use the whole affair for professional purposes; and the Pope seeks to perform his duty as God's appointed judge. As events took place they unfolded like novels of possibility, where incidents occurred through the apparent randomness of personal intervention or chance reaction; now, however, things are perceived in retrospect, through formulations which suggest patterns of inevitability, particularly for each speaker's own involvement. The point of the poet's announced attitudes in book one seems not, therefore, that absolutes exist in order to predetermine moral success as if in some cosmic comedy – Pompilia after all dies,

Caponsacchi fails to save her and Guido is executed unrepentant, a
victim to the end – but rather that moral awareness persists as part
of human psychology, contributing to the dramas of individual
consciousness. Characters draw from a similar store of images,
which means that the same paradigm exists throughout, persisting
through all attempts to reallocate players within its form. Whatever
judgement is made, the function of a universal pattern which
separates good from evil remains. This is Robert Langbaum's point
when he says that Browning in this poem 'goes so far as to bring back
the mythical pattern . . . of the Andromeda story . . . as inherent
in the very structure of the mind, in what we would nowadays call
the unconscious'.[8] Still, the intensity of the drama lies less in the
force of unconscious impetus than in the struggles of consciousness to
understand its place in a scheme which ironically it must perceive
for itself. The moral instruction in book one is simply an extension of
Browning's usual embodiment of his views through unconscious
irony; it is not a recurring plan which reproduces itself in the actions
of men and women, of the sort which is foretold in *Paradise Lost*, but
an instruction about patterns being used to define experience and
moral meaning. In this way Browning creates the structural irony of
moral clarity within a general diffusion of purpose.

As well as providing images for moral discrimination, a paradigm
may suggest a model for emulation, and therefore the proffering of
absolutes is also an aspect of the poem's concern with imitative
action. The histrionic act of resuscitation produces a mimic world,
and in so far as each speaker makes an imitated reality we are
confronted with the way metaphors and constructions of language
essentially form simulations and models. To perceive a pattern in
experience is to make a model which may influence future action as
well as explain the past, and suggestions about example or influence
abound throughout. Among many instances, Half-Rome uses
Guido's actions as a moral fable which supports himself and will act,
he hopes, as a warning to his wife's lover; the Other Half-Rome uses
classical allusions as metaphors for comparing behaviour; Pompilia
is influenced by the old rhyme about the virgin and the paynims;
Caponsacchi was encouraged to emulate his great uncle; the Pope
discusses the force of precedent; Guido argues that the Pope is
bound by tradition to follow St Peter's thought, and complains that
he is himself being executed as an example to Rome. Amidst this
cacophany of assertions about the force of influence, truth like
reality becomes dispersed among varieties of reasoning, and value

becomes a matter of judgement and discrimination among models. The moral challenge faced by the Pope as the man who judges is thus a challenge about influence and quality of action rather than truth of perception. It is a point already observed by David Shaw: the Pope moves towards 'the pragmatic formula that whatever works is conceptually respectable', and he believes that 'when religion, like science, deals with ultimate things, it uses imaginative models, not "facts"', and so when he considers the myths used by both science and religion, it is not for the Pope 'a question of eliminating rhetoric, but only of which model to choose'.[9] Consequently the Pope does not approve of Caponsacchi as an example of the new man, 'the first experimentalist / In the new order of things', since he is guided by his 'own mere impulse' instead of making the church 'rule his law of life' (x.1910-14). The crucial question for the Pope is whether Caponsacchi can teach others 'how to quit themselves, / Show why this step was right while that were wrong' (x.1922-3), and making the heart the source of instruction clearly justifies a Paolo or a Guido as well as a Caponsacchi. Since personal intuition is therefore unreliable, the Christian story of the incarnation and God's loving self-sacrifice is for the Pope the best model for moral experience, both as an explanation of pain which was designed to develop 'The moral qualities of man' and as a guide to action which will lead man to imitate God himself:

> To make him love in turn and be beloved,
> Creative and self-sacrificing too,
> And thus eventually God-like . . .   (x.1381-3)

God is less important for the truth of his existence than for his function as a model to be emulated. In conformity with his self-determined task, the Pope enforces the necessity for judgement, 'Life's business being just the terrible choice' (x.1238), but judgement of value as distinct from judgement of truth. He finds the 'tale' of God's love 'credible' (x.1349), and whether it is a 'fact' or 'only truth reverberate' is not crucial – 'What matter so intelligence be filled?' (x.1388-99). The Pope thus echoes Browning's formulation in the 'Epilogue' to *Dramatis Personae* that truth is not to be found through abstract analysis, but through a demonstration of function. What matters is consciousness of effect, not explanation of cause (x.1400-6), and the responsive action which that consciousness generates:

A thing existent only while it acts,
Does as designed, else a nonentity, –
For what is an idea unrealized?   (x.1501–3)

But Browning does not leave us with the Pope's truth of function, for Guido's second speech follows and implicitly questions the Pope's views by echoing them in another context. Guido also takes a pragmatic approach, being concerned with the expediency of what works and attempting to be whatever he thinks will sustain his life, and he claims that he did indeed do as designed. Through this monologue Browning establishes an ironic counterpoint to the Pope's Christian duty by providing Guido with protestations that challenge the Pope's assumed principles. Guido takes up the pattern of Christian moral conflict, for example, and flaunts his assigned place within it in order to mock its absolutism:

Abate, cross your breast and count your beads
And exorcize the devil, for here he stands
And stiffens in the bristly nape of neck,
Daring you drive him hence!   (xi.554–7)

Villains are ordinary men, not the horny-headed devils of Christian melodrama. Guido's claims, that he has lost individual freedom and been made a victim of social and providential fate, evoke the old conflict between free will and predestination which lurks behind his main argument that he fulfilled God's purpose by being true to his nature as God made him. Through his mocking claim to devilry and wolfishness, he implicitly challenges the whole idea of predetermined roles and assigned judgements, for if he is to be labelled a devil in the Christian moral plot of good versus evil, then he is as necessary to the fulfilment and actualising of that plan as those who play the saviour. The provision of models which influence and define ethical behaviour is accompanied by the problem, which Guido exploits, that villains are as justified as heroes, since they are equally necessary for the realising of a moral idea. Guido may then be right to resent the sense that he has been defined as the third person in someone else's fiction of heroism, conceived as the pawn of some already formulated plot. In all this, however, it is Guido's denial of psychological freedom that is most threatening to the Pope's philosophy, since choice is fundamental to the Pope's hopes for human development. Only in the acceptance of choice, the Pope implies through his own exercise of judgement, is there an acceptance of moral responsibility; otherwise, like Guido, men may succumb instead to a blind inevitability.

The focus and therefore the solution to these ironies lies in the way Browning represents them as psychological conflicts, for inevitability is something Guido perceives when looking back. In him Browning dramatises the ironic result of imposing a pattern on past experience which would deny freedom of choice. The final irony of Guido's character is that it is he who predetermines himself as the victim of moral design, not by choosing to fulfil the role of evil, but, paradoxically, by pretending not to choose the role. By accepting the Pope's wolf image as a description of his naturalness, and by directing his energies to an expediency which depends on how other people view him, he of necessity places himself among the terms of public morality, becoming the puppet of other people's volition or third person of their narrative pattern. In believing that God must have had a purpose for him (xi.2301–3), and therefore not choosing any for himself, he commits himself to a form of psychological abdication, to existing only as a pretended act, because transferring identity to the terms of someone else's fiction, whether God's, the Pope's or even Pompilia's.

Browning does not really need God as 'the prop for his moral being', which has been suggested,[10] because he can demonstrate the varying functions of moral perception within individual character. In writing a series of lengthy monologues, he seems more concerned to explore the psychology of authentic action than the theology of moral truth. In this poem universals can be no more than a human dramatisation, which is underlined by the epistemological irony of the text that ' "God is true / And every man a liar" ' (xii.600–1). In enunciating that text and claiming its truth, Fra Celestino makes himself either God or in terms of its content a liar. But the logic is hardly the point, as Browning suggests by having Bottini notice the irony in order to reject the statement as mere political expediency (xii.647–55). Such texts function not as logical truths, but as psychological affirmations, in this instance asserting the value of an idealism which conceives absolute truth as the necessary concomitant to human falsehood. The way Caponsacchi and the Pope are portrayed suggests that claims to a truthful understanding of experience only attain validity in terms of the struggle towards personal integrity, an independently determined self-conception which is substantiated in some form of action, whether

Caponsacchi's defiance of the court or the Pope's exercise of judgement. The protean potential of self-awareness may lead to moral ambiguity or confusion of purpose, and that is the general state of men as Browning portrays them; yet he also seems to imply that an authentic identity may arise from the independent consciousness which is made possible through self-dramatisation. The re-enacting of past selves or the dramatising of possibility may free personality from the domination of false images, as well as reinforce them. That is not, however, to make the poem a manual for successful living. It is simply that Caponsacchi's independence in court, and the Pope's insistence on judging, are signs of hope in a poem where truths of experience and truths of reality seldom coincide. While histrionic action in *The Ring and the Book* is about the transformations of experience which create individual realities, at the same time I think Browning intended the structure which predetermines an evaluation of its participants to affirm the value of a conscious humanism, however subjective, histrionically generated or ironically conceived that value may be.

6 Experience as Pageant: Subjectivism in *Fifine at the Fair*

Fifine at the Fair is dominated by the speaker's vigour. He pursues the myriad images and intellectual distinctions which flood his mind with an intensity and energy seldom found even among Browning's usually prolix personae. While the result may seem to be a verbal density, obscure in meaning and indeterminate in purpose, this fecundity of mind also produces a verbal display whose gymnastic agility is the mental counterpart of the fairground 'tumbling-troup'.[1] Hovering between obscurity and brilliance, Don Juan finds in the gaiety and artifice of the fair an appropriate context for his attempt to determine the reality of a fleeting, sporadic existence. He draws on images from this backdrop, and from the life around him, to illuminate and extend his argument; in doing so he becomes, in effect, a man turning experience into a form of pageant, someone transforming sensation into a passing parade of the mind's imaginings.

Sensory experience is fundamental to Juan's life, and his interest in Fifine reveals its basic insistence; nevertheless, his debate is a serious effort to locate his most significant and valuable experience in the realm of subjective vision. Sensory data, being merely elemental, is material to be transmuted into his soul's world. All essence, all value and beauty depend on the 'breath' which evokes them, on the individual 'seeing soul'; the world is inert until man evokes its beauty (LV). Juan argues, for example, that the potentialities dormant in the inert world may be realised through the transforming ability of artistic skill, the sculptor's 'hand-practice', or of romantic idealisation, 'soul-proficiency' in love (L); he also believes that the character of each soul is defined by what it gains from this process (LV). What is important for him is the act of transformation itself. It does not matter where the 'elemental flame' springs from,[2] whether from 'gums and spice' or 'straw and rottenness', as long as the 'soul has power to make them burn' (LV), to transfer the latent essences in the physical world, all that is 'achieved in visible things', into a realm of the 'soul's imaginings' (LVI).[3] But resonant throughout the poem is the underlying question of what sort of reality these imaginings attain, and since the process of transformation amounts to the soul's creation of itself through interaction with the external world, the problem is allied to Juan's concern with the reality of his own existence. Imaginings are by nature illusory and amidst the fertile show of imaginative perception into which all is transposed what substance does he himself have? Is he, too, illusory?[4] Can he validate his subjective vision, or is sensory experience the only reality and his metaphysics mere imaginings? These issues, the definition of his soul's world and the concomitant fabric of his own being, are explored through discussions of pageants and drama, through arguing the reality of illusion.

Juan, as a subjectivist, develops his monologues by exploiting the conditions of his subjectivity. He does not deny or deplore the pervasive deceptions in life, but in order to explain his view of existence he deliberately exploits the artifices which subsist in all human affairs. To develop the implications of a series of images, then, as he does,[5] is perfectly in keeping with his understanding of being, since the images are *simulacra*, the illusion not the reality, and they directly embody the nature of the world 'i' the soul' (LIV). It is appropriate, therefore, that he regards experience as a pageant, as something which is acted or simulated, and it is also appropriate, of course, that fairs should play such a dominant role in his deliberations, both the literal fair of Pornic which he walks through, and the metaphorical fair of Venice in his dream.[6] In discussing these fairs, and in discussing the device of an imaginative pageant of women and the artifice of drama, he is preoccupied with the ways in which illusion may embody reality and truth. His task is to distil from the illusion its essential validity, and to handle the deception without being corrupted by it.

The necessity for manipulating artifice is perhaps best illustrated in Juan's swimming metaphor, whose implications impinge on his attention to life's pageant-like qualities. He compares swimming, the fruitless attempt to rise from water and remain in air, to his 'spirit's life / 'Twixt false, whence it would break, and true, where it would bide' (LXV). Just as a swimmer must learn to work with the 'obstructing' medium he finds himself in, and not fight against it, so

man must endure and work with the medium of deception or, like
the swimmer, be consumed by it. By deceiving, Juan learns to
master deception, and thence to perceive the truth in falsehood. He
also develops an extraordinary capacity for handling appearances,
which is necessary if man is to understand the nature and function of
their façade:

> Full well I know the thing I grasp, as if intent
> To hold, – my wandering wave, – will not be grasped at all:
> The solid-seeming grasped, the handful great or small
> Must go to nothing, glide through fingers fast enough;
> But none the less, to treat liquidity as stuff –
> Though failure – certainly succeeds beyond its aim,
> Sends head above, past thing that hands miss, all the same.
>
>   (LXVI)

The paradox lies in his exercise of pretence: he practises self-
delusion by treating a liquid as if it were a solid. This act naturally
fails, but it nevertheless allows sufficient success to ensure his
survival. Truth is obtained through designed and controlled
deception, with the consequence that the validity of his argument
depends on his intellectual nimbleness in handling illusion.[7]

Sometimes the mental acrobatics may seem like a performance
which inflates the trivial, mere virtuoso exercises, particularly since
their primary purpose is to defend the liaison with a prostitute; and
certainly an air of gay exuberance, verging on frivolity, pervades
the poem. Perhaps his debate is simply a semantic romp – how a
subjectivist substantiates his existence, or how someone who might
not exist proves that he does. Such a problem easily becomes an
intellectual sport (played here with vigorous verbal artifice), but it
also has ultimately serious consequences, for Browning as well as for
any Don Juan wishing to justify sexual dalliance which provokes
connubial discord. While it might appear that the ambiguities in a
parade of deception would obscure philosophical speculation,
recognition of the function of such ambiguities may also lead to an
understanding of the kind of truth available to man, both in art and
in life. The paradox of Juan's achievement is that through the
conscious flaunting of artifice he formulates and embodies a
'histrionic truth'. This last phrase emerges from his discussion of
Fifine as an actress (LXXXV), and it was his interest in drama which
impelled his walk through the Pornic fair (LXXXVII).

As Roma King has said, 'the poem seeks some abiding truth amid the dissolving fragments of the external world; specifically, the speaker gropes for reality of self and, by extension, for the reality of a changeless order beyond time'.[8] But the speaker's quest for these realities is characterised by his self-dependent method; it is the consciously subjective manner of Juan's quest (his exploitation of artifice) which, I suggest, gives the poem its uniqueness. The quality of the poem's texture is the quality of Juan's experience and that experience is inseparable from his flirtation with illusion, from the nature of a pageant. The typical process of his mind, which treats sensory experience as a series of images to be pondered over and manipulated, may be seen in the opening sections as he moves from description of the situation to questioning its meaning. The result is an uncertain mixture of tangibility and abstraction, where the tangibility of the scene is continually undermined, frequently by some deliberate verbal strategy. Fifine, for instance, in the section following her initial appearance becomes 'a phantom', a 'Sexless and bloodless sprite' (xvi). The poem's dialectic is thus more complicated than previous argumentative poems such as 'Bishop Blougram's Apology'. The sense of abstraction there results from the way the Bishop's images are mostly hypothetical analogies, appropriated because suitable to his argument rather than because they arise from an environment which impinges on his consciousness. Juan's sensual life is more acute and many of his images, embodying his sensory experience, emerge directly from his surroundings; these images intermingle with other images supplied from the memory or the imagination, and with mental reflection, providing an intimate relationship between experience and response, or between experience of sensation and experience of mind. The involvement of mind with sensation characterises experience for most of Browning's monologuists, but it is Juan's consciousness of the process which makes him distinctive. More than any of Browning's characters he is aware of the interweaving of perception and conceptualising. Therefore the chequered, shifting degrees of tangibility and abstraction are an intended effect of the poem's verbal quality and part of his attempt to understand and explain the nature of his own consciousness as well as life's deceptive appearances. His play with pageants and illusion is thus an elaboration of his subjectivism. I propose now to examine the details of Juan's preoccupation with fairs, and then to discuss the limitations of his vision, since his 'histrionic truth', the illusory reality of his imaginings, combines both his success and his failure.

There are four distinctive forms of pageant in the poem: the Pornic fair, the procession of women, Fifine's stage-drama and the Venetian fair in Juan's dream. The Pornic fair is the first of these and Juan's monologue opens with his enthusiasm for the sudden appearance of the gypsies who produce it. Their nature and behaviour manifest various issues which trouble his more sophisticated mind. He immediately delights, for instance, in their manner of transforming things: the fair grew from 'Mere bit of hoarding . . . as brisk as butterfly from grub' (ii); 'squalid girls' are 'transformed to gamesome boys' (iii); and the caravan itself burst from a bud into the 'queen-tulip of the Fair!' (iv). However, he soon focuses on their moral independence, which he obviously regards with some sympathy. Having left society for 'free life, full liberty!' (vii), they have no respect for reputation or good fame. They exploit fairground illusion (this year's 'six-legged sheep' was last year's 'Twin-headed Babe, and Human Nondescript!'; xi), and they care nothing for social disapproval of such fraud. Juan, sharing their desire for lawlessness (vi), is fascinated by this inversion of social mores: 'How comes it, all we hold so dear they count so cheap?' (x). He also notices that despite their physical and moral independence they do not divorce themselves completely from the community, for they return to sell their wares. The paradox in the gypsies' situation is that their freedom is limited by the requirements of physical survival: 'They, of the wild, require some touch of us the tame, / Since clothing, meat and drink, mean money all the same' (viii). At this stage of the poem, the implications of this paradox are not clear, but Juan's intellectual argument will eventually involve a similar dilemma: his ontological independence is circumscribed by the necessity for other people to acknowledge and thereby sustain his existence. The gypsies' freedom, supported through contact with others and by means of artifice and deceit, provides an appropriate physical context for the initiation of this more abstract contemplation.

Fifine herself culminates the opening sections of the Pornic fair, since she epitomises what is most alluring in the lawless character of her people: she is 'self-sustainment made morality' (xvi). Her ethical nature emerges from her essential being; it is a natural affair, not bound by the contrivances of social convention. She is 'free and flower-like, with loveliness for law'. Such independence of spirit and action appeals to Juan, but her naturalness is threatening as well as enticing. She is also 'mischievous and mean' (xvi). She evokes not only the dangerous excitement inherent in what is illicit, but also the more subtle, tantalising mixture of enchantment and fear which is promised by unknown and unconventional experiences. This combination of allure and threat both titillates the senses and provokes a challenge of mind which Juan cannot resist – a challenge illustrated in the image of a lily which attracts insects to their death by 'devices' such as scent (xvii). The fault, Juan implies, lies in the victim, in the deceived rather than the deceiver, in whoever is unable to discriminate. He assumes for himself, of course, a superior wisdom which perceives both the charm and the hazard, and which is therefore able to admire at a distance, to 'peer and praise' discreetly, putting 'rich things to right use' (xviii). This claim underlies his whole concern with artifice. Though yet to be fully articulated, the point is that deception is not simply immoral; it needs to be acknowledged and handled, as 'self-sustainment' for the insect means recognition of the lily's device. These opening sections (i–xviii), presenting the context of the Pornic fair, are introductory in character and the least explicit in explaining Juan's interest in pageants, but already the capacity for managing illusion becomes vital, for it enables him to distinguish value and to realise reality.

In the second form of pageant, the imagined procession of women, Juan pursues his subjective view of things by openly developing an illusory event; sustaining the act of fancy for twenty-one sections (xix–xxxix), he exploits this parade of traditional female beauty in order to show Elvire his vision of her, his perception of her value. Of course, it should not be forgotten that Juan's metaphysics begin first with physics, and as he introduces the women his usual delight in fleshly surfaces is quickly apparent, particularly in his description of Cleopatra (xx). However, conscious of his attention to sensual detail and of its effect on Elvire, he atones for his indulgence by placing her with her peers in the parade, where she will 'prove best of beauty there!' (xxiii). Important to his purpose is his distinction between the phantoms in his fancy and the reality nearby. When Elvire joined the line, she gave up her 'clog/Of flesh' (xxiii), and he pursues a perception of two Elvires, one beside him and one in the pageant, to enable Elvire to observe herself more easily. Two female phantoms, Elvire and Fifine, though 'mere/Illusion . . . dream-figures', are to be judged by Juan and Elvire, 'the true' (xxvi). A common enough exercise of the imagination, allowing an individual to make a detached self-appraisal, this artifice enables Juan to distinguish between the realities of flesh and spirit. (It indicates also his attempt to objectify his subjective experience, and to bring Elvire to do the same.) He does not revere the flesh unduly, he says, because his main interest lies in 'the inward grace' which is reached 'through the outward sign' (xxvIII), a statement which is central to the truth he seeks to embody in this masque. He believes that 'quick sense' is able to perceive the 'Self-vindicating flash' in each man and woman (xxIx). Each person has an essential and unique value, yet the kind and degree of value is always to be determined, and the subjectivity of Juan's position is indicated by the way even a person's 'inward grace', or essence, depends on how it is construed by another.

A description of Elvire culminates the pageant, establishing the nature of her value for her husband. She stands 'pure' in 'pale constraint', 'Inviolate of life and worldliness and sin'; there is a slow, languid quality about her appearance; her clothes protectively mask her virginal beauty, and despite her 'rebellious' breasts the whole effect is one of statuesque calm (xxxvIII). Though the calm hints at lifelessness – the dress is a 'pall' – and Elvire's anaemic aspect is quite antithetical to Fifine's provocative challenge, Juan still urges the sincerity of his admiration: she 'makes right and whole once more/All that was half itself without' her (xxxIx). Elvire, of course, is astonished at his description, since her mirror reflects ' "a tall, thin, pale, deep-eyed/Personage" ' (xL), and apparently forgetting his separation of the two Elvires, she asks him where 'i' the world' all this 'wonder' is found.

In one sense the artifice of the pageant conceals reality, since it diverts attention from the true, or real, to the false, or fictional (see xxvI), and Juan earlier says how such pageants once screened the grave from Louis xI, hiding his impending death (xIx). But Juan's use of this fictive device also clarifies reality, the reality of subjective evaluation – the soul's perception. This reality is abstract (illusory in quality), and in response to Elvire's question, which concludes direct elaboration of the pageant, he turns to art as his evidence 'That something was, is, might be; but no more thing itself,/Than flame is fuel' (xLI). Though this statement may seem even more enigmatic than the reality he seeks to describe, it provides a basis for the discussion of transformation which it precedes, and it infers the pageant-like substance of his consciousness. Flame arises from fuel and is inextricably related to the fuel, but the two are distinct in type and attribute. Similarly, the response to a work of art, the beauty born from it, is ontologically distinct from the original art-object. If Juan tries to 'test fancy in [his] brain/By fact which gave it birth', he fails, he says, 'to find that vision of delight' (XLII). Though we may perhaps now be more adept at explaining cause in art and find his aesthetics naive, nevertheless the problem is still pertinent, particularly when he refers to music – why *do* we find beauty in enharmonic modulation? The answer, Juan suggests, lies in the soul's transmuting power, in imaginative insight, that act which transforms inert matter into subjective vision. Yet this vision, or beauty, the response to art, has no tangible substance in itself; it is no 'thing itself', being of the mind, and the pageant of women, as a delineated fancy, is a similar order of experience. After elaborating further the soul's transforming ability, and developing the swimming metaphor to demonstrate the importance of artifice (which I referred to earlier), Juan suggests more fully the nature of such an indeterminate fabric by explaining the value of dramatic illusion; this explanation constitutes his next main focus on forms of pageant.

As night approaches, the literal ocean before Juan recedes into the enveloping dusk; 'its plash and plaint' seem to retire, 'as if their part/Were played' (LXXXIV). The dramatic image is important, for it indicates the way physical reality passes through his mind like scenes in a pageant, and it prepares for his comments on drama. Admiration for acting, he suggests, is caused by 'our hate of falsehood' and by the 'mere part, things play' (LXXXV). Drama is applauded because it is an acknowledged, not a covert, artifice, the point which Mr Sludge always conveniently neglected. 'We also act', Juan says, pointing to the constant simulation in life, but only actors preface their performance with ' "A lie is all we do or say" ', and therein rests the paradoxical value of dramatic art. 'To feign, means – to have grace/And so get gratitude!' A crucial point, however, is the need to recognise the illusion, to distinguish between the object and its imitation; otherwise all enjoyment is lost: 'Mistake [the actor's] false for true, one minute, – there's an end/Of the admiration!' There is a difference, then, between aesthetic experience and real experience:

> Truth, we grieve at or rejoice:
> 'T is only falsehood, plain in gesture, look and voice,
> That brings the praise desired, since profit comes thereby.
> (LXXXV)

'Truth', actual experience, demands a committed response; it is not to be admired so much as accepted or acted upon. Discernible falsehood requires the observer to distinguish between the real and the simulated, consequently allowing him to admire the skill and success of the artifice. However, actual experience may also require recognition of illusion, and this exercise of the mind which drama requires is not merely some facile, pleasurable act; it also involves a more serious tenet: 'The histrionic truth is in the natural lie' (LXXXV). This complement of oxymorons forms Juan's key paradox. On one level, it simply means that artistic truth resides in the acknowledgement of its falsehood: an artifice is an artifice. But it also has a more profound meaning, which rests on the opposition between 'histrionic' and 'natural'. 'Histrionic truth', the truth contained in art, in consciously designed artifice or in that which is dramatised, is concomitant with the 'natural lie', the falsehood which permeates all natural things (natural implies all that is not contrived – man himself and the world of nature he inhabits). Everything, Juan says, 'has a false outside, whereby a truth is forced/To issue from within' (LXXXVI), and art would seem to be truthful, therefore, because it provides an analogue for that paradox. Artistic truth, however, is not merely a model for reality; nor is it a question of being more real or less real than life; it is inextricable from the truth about life. Illusion characterises both art and life, requiring careful discrimination for the proper understanding and appreciation of each, and consequently the kind of truth available to man in art, the artifice of a dramatised illusion, parallels the kind of truth available to man in life, the artifice of a natural lie. They are twin mirrors, each reflecting the other.

This passage (LXXXV – LXXXVI) is the climax of Juan's progress to this point. The drama paradox is not simply abstract speculation; it emerges from the inner qualities of his character, indicating his aesthetic sensibility and the histrionic, pageant-like texture of his experience. His liking for 'the honest cheating' provoked his walk through the Pornic fair to see 'the strollers on their stage' (LXXXVII), and the drama metaphor becomes the focal point for his insistence on the necessity and value of handling illusion; it justifies his interest in artifice, and in Fifine, who demands the exercise of his discriminating faculties. It also explains the importance of his agility of mind, since all he says rests on the reliability of his mental discrimination, an assumption which underlies his argument throughout. As in drama, where success is lost if the false is mistaken for true, so in Juan's performance, if he mistakes false for true, the validity of his thought is similarly lost. The truth in his discourse, then, lies in its histrionic, subjective substance, in his overt flaunting of artifice.

Juan next introduces a dream he had earlier in the morning. Perplexed and overwhelmed after a swim by 'fancies manifold' and 'memories new and old' (LXXXIX), he reverted to music for the 'Truth that escapes prose' (XC). He played Schumann's *Carnaval*, reflecting on the 'certainty of change', the falsehood to be found in art as in nature (XCIII), and slipped into a dream where Pornic and Schumann merge and are transformed into a Venetian Fair. The dream is the last of his forms of pageant and represents the ubiquity of illusion. In the Venetian Fair, a 'Concourse immense of men and women' all masked, the human condition becomes a maze of disguise, where the only known reality is the disguise itself: each person makes 'the vizard whence himself should view the world, / And where the world believed himself was manifest' (XCV). Since the dream is a visual emblem only, without sound, Juan attains truth by observing these masks, the *simulacra* which represent each human identity; he has to regard appearances, elicit 'truth by what men seemed, not said' (C). He also discovers that shifting his position from above the fair to within its midst produces a change in his attitude towards the crowd. From above, the faces in the crowd seemed 'crook'd / And clawed away from God's prime purpose', but at close range the 'brutality' is easier to accept (XCIX), as is also the 'wrong' in men (CI). Through the strength of his will, therefore, he could 'pick and choose':

> Determine to observe, or manage to escape,
> Or make divergency assume another shape
> By shift of point of sight in me the observer.   (CI)

By shifting the observer he alters what is observed, and thus Juan discovers the role of the subject in perception. The episode shows that 'one must abate / One's scorn of the soul's casing', learn to evaluate, not deride, surface illusion, since the outward mask is the physical container for what might otherwise perish (CII). Comparing his delight in watching the crowd with the elation of a chemist who constructs a hypothetical reality, the diversity of life 'in fancy', by seeking a principle of causation beyond surface effects, Juan says he thus gluts his hunger to 'be' and 'know' what he is, by contrast with what he is not, and therefore 'through sham/And outside', he arrives 'at inmost real' (CIII). That is the function of illusion and the passage indicates again Juan's subjective penetration of façades, his apprehension of a histrionic truth constructed in 'fancy'. It also represents Browning's interest in the attributes of personality which lie behind outward, potentially misleading appearances, in the psychological reality which is to be discovered through dramatised artifice, both in life and art.

Juan's dream-vision soon undergoes 'A formidable change' (CV). Before his gaze, the square in Venice expands its significance to symbolise first Europe and then the world: the Venetian Carnival is 'the state/Of mankind' (CVIII). From this knowledge, he says, it is easy to infer the meaning of his altered attitude towards the 'brute-pageant'. Once he left his 'pride of place' above the crowd and reached the ground, he discovered that he could explain the 'glories by the shames/Mixed up in man, one stuff miscalled by different names'. The important point is to 'get close enough!' (CVIII). Through direct contact with the fairground illusion, with 'mimes/And mummers', he could balance the contradictions and understand man's paradoxical nature (CVIII). To become acquainted with 'the way o' the world', we need, he says, to 'bid a frank farewell to what – we think – should be', and 'welcome what is – we find' (CIX). Juan's preoccupation with pageants has been an effort to describe both life's deceptions and the nature of his consciousness; it has also been an endeavour to explain the need for involvement with the pageant (on a physical plane with Fifine; on a metaphysical plane with the reality of illusion), for while life's surfaces may be a mask, the meaning of the masquerade can only be understood through handling it, through personal experience. In other words, meaning depends on the subjectivity of his point of view, which is clear from his emphasis on the difference between looking at the Venetian Fair from above and viewing it from within its midst, and from the manipulation of his position within the fair, holding 'the balance', shifting 'The weight from scale to scale' (CVIII).

The whole epistemological issue is characterised by its embodiment in the events of a dream. The Venetian Fair indicates the ephemeral carnival of life, but as its forms are further undermined by change, their illusion liable even to total dissolution ('shadow sucked the whole/*Facade* into itself'; CX), the 'strange scene-picture' (CXVIII) becomes a series of passing episodes which, as images in a dream, represent the pageant-like experience of Juan's mind. The dream, then, dramatises his subjectivism. Life's representation as a masquerade within a dream, subject to the strange transformation of dreams, symbolises his imaginative perception of things. The physical world in relation to the soul's world thus becomes a fiction within an illusion, or a pageant within a pageant, where the truth of the soul's. world is similar in kind to that of drama – a 'histrionic truth', which is a counterpart to the 'natural lie' of the physical world. This relationship is directly presented when Juan's dream and his walk with Elvire both conclude at a Druid monument. Bringing together literal object and dream image, Juan is able to portray in one climactic symbol the interplay between sensory perception and imaginative insight, where the enigmas of the monument's physical presence (CXXII), and folk speculation about it (CXXIII), underlie and reinforce the metaphysical paradoxes which it represents in his dream (CXXIV). As the 'Sole object' which remains identifiable before him and Elvire, unconsumed by 'twilight's hungry jaw' (CXXII), the literal stones parallel their incorporeal counterpart, the 'mammoth-stones' which become the one 'common shape' of his dissolving dream (CXX, CXXIV).

There is, however, another dimension to Juan's position. His manipulation of Elvire in directing her to the Druid monument so that its physical presence before her coincided with its metaphorical presence in his dream (CXXI), and his general exercise of artifice in elaborating the various pageants, point to a premeditated design in his monologue. As I have suggested, Juan's awareness of his procedure is vital. He realises that the ego exists in a world of appearances (indicated by the fairground context) and that any effort to reason about existence must consequently be founded on illusion. The soul's world and consciousness of the soul's world are of the mind, and so of the order of fiction. He emphasises, therefore, a mind-dependent existence which is illusory in quality, and it is his flaunting of these fictive conditions of consciousness which distinguishes him from previous monologuists. He has a more refined self-consciousness, which leads both to his success, enabling him to assert 'the value of a lie' (CXXIV), a paradox of considerable significance for Browning's art, and to his failure, revealing the limitations in 'histrionic truth', in a subjectivist philosophy.

The emphasis on his self-consciousness means that like the Duke of Ferrara he is egocentric, but it does not mean that like the Duke he wills 'the extinction of every other self'.[9] Rather, he develops a solipsistic position, where other selves are unreal compared with his own existence. In the midst of the pageant of life, he needs to convince himself that his soul, while also pageant-like in its illusory quality, is nevertheless a reality, and the function of other souls is to provide this assurance: 'Down underneath the show, we put forth hand and pluck/At what seems somehow like reality – a soul' (LXVII). As part of the pageant, this other soul also proves illusory, and any consideration for it is easily dismissed ('come who knows whence, gone gaily who knows where!'). Yet it 'did its duty', and confirmed his existence. His words – 'I felt it, it felt me' – suggest duplicity, but any literal meaning is countered, at least initially, by the metaphorical level of his thought as he asserts the solipsist's attitude:

> The main point is – the false fluidity was bound
> Acknowledge that it frothed o'er substance, nowise found
> Fluid, but firm and true.   (LXVII)

Several sections later, in response to Elvire's objection that he seeks such confirmation only from women, he repeats the claim. Women, by disengaging his soul from 'the shows of things', prove his existence. They convince him that he is a 'truth, though all else seem/And be not' (LXXX), and thus establish him as the centre of his own universe, or 'the still point of the turning world', to anticipate the *Four Quartets*:

> The falsity, beside, is fleeting: I can stand
> Still, and let truth come back, – your steadying touch of hand
> Assists me to remain self-centred, fixed amid
> All on the move.   (LXXX)

Women do this because they are capable of self-sacrifice; men cannot because they are more concerned with self-gratification (Juan attacks man as a horrible putrescence who is moved by envy rather than by love; LXXIX). These sections on male and female principles (LXIX–LXXX), culminating in the serious point about proving his reality, dazzle in their verbal virtuosity, but the perplexity for the reader lies in the degree of Juan's awareness about several implications of his argument. He ignores the possible intrusion of sensory experience ('felt' and 'touch'). He appears oblivious to the reflexive effect of his scorn for man's impotent love:

if man is an egocentric whose 'love-apple' is a 'stinted crab', then by gender so is Juan. And he ignores particularly the parasitical implications in his relationship with women, which severely modify the proposition of his soul's independence. His clear statements of feminine sacrifice – a woman 'Takes nothing and gives all' (LXXX) – suggest he does realise these anomalies, and perhaps the intensity of his attack on men in section LXXIX partly reflects a furious frustration with his own impotence in being unable to prove his reality without external assistance. He cannot openly confess these matters, because they would detract from his concern with self-definition. But, whether or not Browning intended to imply Juan's silent recognition of them at this particular point, they do indicate a serious flaw in Juan's discourse: he has reduced love to a means of masculine aggrandisement. It is a qualitative restriction, suggesting that selfish pride is an inevitable corollary of his self-reliant methods. 'Self-sustainment made morality' becomes a self-centred exercise in self-approval. What Juan fails to consider is that any proof of his own existence through the 'touch' of some other soul may also prove the reality of that other soul, which result would obviously deny his solipsism. His not reflecting on this possibility suggests that his emphasis on a fictional, mind-dependent existence, while intellectually viable, is a matter of personal convenience, and these unconsidered implications in Juan's argument indicate, I think, the limitations in his debate.

That they are limitations intended by Browning is clear when Juan himself eventually recognises his faults. After his penetration into the 'principle of things' at the Druid stones (CXXIV), he is unable to sustain such heights of metaphysical confidence and he descends from the metaphorical veil of reality to the physical veil of Fifine (CXXV). As he 'disengaged' the former, so he hints at surreptitious lifting of the latter. The travesty is inevitable, because despite his emphasis on subjective vision he can never deny sensation, and the struggle to free himself from the realities – and moralities – of the flesh will always fail. Like the swimmer, he must remain in the water, however far out of it he manages to reach. All new experience ultimately leads back to the same commonplace ground it started from (CXXVI), and his awareness of this circular movement provokes a sense of weary futility, whose aching tiredness ends only with the peace of death (CXXVII).

Juan, subdued by this unpromising thought, is then impressed with the notion that 'each lie' has 'Redounded to the praise of man'

(CXXVIII). The limitation in his argument, he realises, was that his exercise of mind was flattering to his pride, merely asserting the power of his personal will; 'and Truth, unlike the False with Truth's outside,/Neither plumes up his will nor puffs him out with pride'. Pure truth would be free from personal vanity because objective, and Juan's highly wrought attempts to register the qualities of his experience have been an effort to objectify his own subjective processes. But he senses here that he has not succeeded and his previous insight is rendered doubtful, even suspiciously like some instinctive assertion of his self-importance. Soul has not triumphed as he has been at pains to suggest; rather it is sense which has provoked his argument, since the evidence for sensory perception is available on request – with sense it is 'ask and have'. Sense, he says, promotes self as the soul's only master:

> Such savour in the nose
> Of Sense, would stimulate Soul sweetly, I suppose,
> Soul with its proper itch of instinct, prompting clear
> To recognize soul's self Soul's only master here
> Alike from first to last.   (CXXVIII)

All he has established, he implies, is the power of his own will to deceive himself into believing he is his own master. It is an entirely human illusion to effect, since the soul is not only stimulated by the senses in this act, but also by 'its proper itch of instinct'. Now willing to admit the possibility that some 'soul' other than himself is 'master everywhere', he implies, in another of his cryptic aphorisms, that reality from without is prior to his consciousness and not dependent on his responses: man 'receives/And not demands – not first likes faith and then believes' (CXXVIII). Reality, then, is not entirely mind-dependent, or fictitious in quality, though consciousness of it may be, which is why this belated confession does not finally undercut Juan's previous argument. It was not that he made sophistical claims, but that he claimed too much. His use of pageants to characterise his subjectivism is effective and viable, but when he attempts to subsume all existence within the boundaries of his consciousness he becomes self-indulgent and his objectivity dubious.[10]

Philip Drew has located the central theme of the poem in Juan's statement: '"From the given point evolve the infinite!"' (CXXIX).[11] But this is not the central theme; as Juan says himself, it is his 'problem posed aright', what his task ought to have been. Instead of analysing one spot in depth, he has attempted to extend his inquiry into some endless linear expansion of thought and perception, to 'Fix into one Elvire a Fair-ful of Fifines!' The effort consequently produces a stretching of experience which underlies his attention to the pageantry in life. Just as the existence of a pageant depends on the continuing artifice of its action, so Juan's existence depends on the continuing artifice of his experience. Now, however, as his walk ends where it began (cxxvii), he is confronted with the ironic condition of human consciousness, brought to realise that the extension of experience is circular and reflexive, not linear and expansive; and so he proposes to give up the 'fickle element' (the sea, or his sporting with illusion) to remain with Elvire (cxxix).

This decision, however, depends on the realities of sensation, and if Elvire is to support his existence permanently, she needs herself to be tangible, not some fleeting abstraction, and so the fear that his subjective perception of her may have denied her physical subst-ance produces a sudden, desperate cry for proof of her presence:

> Touch me, and so appear alive to all intents!
> Will the saint vanish from the sinner that repents?
> Suppose you are a ghost! A memory, a hope,
> A fear, a conscience! Quick! Give back the hand I grope
> I' the dusk for!   (cxxx)

When the message from Fifine arrives and the necessary 'touch' remains a possibility from that quarter, then he can dismiss Elvire once more to the realms of idealism, restoring her as a phantasm of the mind: 'slip from flesh and blood, and play the ghost again!' (cxxxii). It is a deft gesture on Browning's part, not undermining Juan as a rank sophist, but revealing the self-determined motivation for his metaphysical brilliance. Sense is indeed the fundamental reality, and ironically Juan is at last objective when he apprehends this – though the insight changes nothing. Morality is of the mind, and therefore an abstraction, subject to the whims of subjectivity. Sense perception, though fundamental and requiring Juan to acknowledge souls other than his own, will not by itself provoke moral action in terms other than his own.

Browning, in *Fifine at the Fair*, has created a persona who pursues an elaborate flirtation with fictions in order to characterise the fabric of consciousness, and this is splendidly achieved through

Juan's treatment of experience as a pageant. However, 'histrionic truth' is both truth and histrionic, and there is still the problem that the passing pageant may be nothing more than a pageant. Juan's subjective discrimination of value and his metaphysical speculation may be an act of self-deception, provoked by sensation in order to convince himself that he was the centre of his existence, to satisfy the demands of instinctive self-indulgence. This possibility becomes Browning's sense of the limitations in a subjectivist philosophy, and just as the gypsies' freedom is limited by their need for contact with society, so is Juan's moral and ontological independence limited by his need for contact with other people. An audience is required to watch the pageant in order to sustain its existence, and that restriction provides both sensory delight and moral culpability.

7 The Self as Subject

Experience for Browning's characters is more than involvement in a merely sensory event or factual incident; it incorporates personal awareness, the interpretation of physical data or the value attached to sensation, and above all the sense that something has happened to the self. This is in accord with general understanding of the term, since 'experience' is defined in one of its aspects by *The Shorter Oxford English Dictionary* as 'the fact of being consciously the subject of a state or condition, or of being consciously affected by an event'. However, to be thus the subject of a situation is to be in an ambiguous if not confusing position, since the subject may be the governing agent, that which performs an action like the grammatical subject of a sentence, or it may instead be a product of the condition, caused by that situation and in effect its object rather than its subject. The crucial factor in experience, though, is consciousness, and to be 'consciously the subject of a state or condition' is to imply that the mind or self is a thinking or active participant, though whether it participates as a defined or defining agent is a fundamentally awkward question.

By writing monologues Browning dramatises experience in this sense of being the conscious subject of an event, and his art is to portray the subtleties of interacting levels and facets of consciousness in the midst of such experience. Also, through irony which undermines the authority of the speaker, questioning the validity of that experience, Browning draws attention to the way it is the speaker's role as subject which is the dramatic focus in the poems; in this any ambivalence about the origins of identity is part of the dramatic conflict. It leads to the obvious moral issue, for instance, that a character whose behaviour is the product of social influences cannot be responsible for what he does, and both Mr Sludge and Guido Franceschini attempt to use such an argument. But Sludge in particular also wants to affirm an independent self which has a validity and humanity otherwise denied by his patrons, and as well as the observation of externally or socially imposed forces there is also the conflicting sense of a self which is self-determining. Browning's speakers frequently become caught within this contradiction – none struggles more than Andrea del Sarto, for example, and even Pippa personifies the Day as providing opportunities which are either 'tasks' imposed on it or 'freaks' at its own pleasure – and consequently one of the recurring conflicts in the monologues is this ambivalent view that man is a self-governing creature and equally that life is controlled by deterministic laws. The dilemma is of course the old Christian humanist problem of individual free will in a universe governed by providence, but for Browning it becomes a psychological drama focused on the realities of individual desires and the fictions of individual rationalisations.

It is possible when confronted with this sort of contention to make a sociological, role-playing interpretation and regard the self as a mask and belief in freedom of action as a functional illusion, a self-deception which is necessary for everyday living. Morse Peckham argues this view when he says that personality to Browning was 'self-conception as self-deception for the sake of arriving at a strategy for action',[1] and certainly the implication in *Pippa Passes* that free will is an illusion or Andrea del Sarto's resort to an illusory choice would appear to provide the evidence. But this behavioural approach makes 'a strategy for action' the goal of the exercise, and therefore emphasises the social dimension of identity at the expense of the internal, personal impetus which is always a force in the poems. In a form where the portrayal of a single perspective draws attention to the strength of individual assertiveness, the speaker's sense of being the subject or central focus of his experience is almost invariably accompanied by an effort to claim some authority over external circumstances, to affirm the essential stability and justice of *his* place. The characteristically persuasive tone, for instance, of various modes of argument, contemplation or declamation in the monologues is a sign of the speaker's desire to impose attitudes on others, to shape experience itself, even within the spontaneity of an ephemeral conversation. Whatever the degree of provocation in the social situation, characters invariably respond to some underlying personal motive, perhaps a need for explanation or for the security of definition, and it is in the sense of this response to internal desire that the monologues are self-generating. Sometimes there may be a shift between the more immediate demands of social expediency and the less necessary development of individual expressiveness. The opening outburst in 'Mr Sludge' is hardly occasioned by a desire to discuss spiritual truth, but the threat of public exposure is still absorbed eventually into a fabric of personal analysis, just as the speakers in *The Ring and the Book* shape the events of the Franceschini murder into versions which fit their own requirements. Consequently the monologue form tends to stress an effort to assert self against the world. For each speaker it is the feeling of himself, of his status as a substantive subject within the world of experience, which he wishes to validate. In this endeavour his own needs are more important than society's. Self-deception may therefore be a means of maintaining an illusion of independent identity more than a strategy for action, and that is a psychological problem of consciousness rather than a sociological concern with behaviour.

Browning's concern with this self-centred authority is to be found from the beginning of his work, even in *Pauline*. There the speaker refers to a clear 'consciousness / Of self' which is linked in him

> to self-supremacy,
> Existing as a centre to all things,
> Most potent to create and rule and call
> Upon all things to minister to it.   (ll. 269–76)

However, by the time Browning reaches *Pippa Passes*, after *Paracelsus*, *Sordello* and the plays, such 'self-supremacy' is portrayed ironically as a solipsistic illusion, and with this shift he introduces the insight that self-conception is an idealism and therefore personality potentially a fiction. Characters are shown striving to sustain the self as a centre around which all else revolves, a 'mimic-monarch' of the universe, to use Browning's image from the 'Epilogue' to *Dramatis Personae*. But while each speaker thinks of himself as the subject or generating force of his own experience, that may only be a convenient illusion and he may be ironically its object instead. The elusiveness which may result from such an ambiguity means that in some poems, such as 'A Death in the Desert', the speaker lacks definition in the more popular sense of personality as idiosyncratic individualism, or eccentric mannerisms which mark someone as 'a real character'. Yet St John affirms an awareness of selfhood despite his loss of vitality: 'I myself remain: I feel myself' (l. 80). He acclaims the importance of fictional conceptualising as a means of attaining spiritual fulfilment, and therefore he is able to articulate a conception of identity which through proposing the hypothesis of a continuing existence provides his consciousness with a defining unity of purpose. He exists, like all Browning's monologuists, in terms of this dramatised conception.

Of course the prospect that the self is a fiction is not the invention of Browning or the nineteenth century. David Hume had already challenged the existence of personality, arguing that only changing impressions are experienced and not any single self; identity is simply a quality of continuity which is ascribed through memory to a succession of perceptions. However, whereas eighteenth-century views like Hume's emphasised memory as the source of identity and the nineteenth century tended to perceive personality in terms of process and growth,[2] Browning's approach to poetic form implies a theory of personality based on a dramatic model: the self as self-dramatised, or the self as the product of a self-reflexive use of language. Retrospection and memory still play their part, but as a contribution to present shaping, the immediate act of consciousness, rather than to continuity with the past. In 'A Death in the Desert' Browning comes closest to describing the nature of personality as a Romantic self with its basis in development and memory, advancing through stages in a world which is a vale of Keatsian soul-making, growing through the 'three souls' of 'what Does', 'what Knows' and 'what Is', in the terms which Browning assigns to 'the gloss of Theotypas' (ll. 82–104). Still, this 'gloss' is to be related in the poem to St John's conception of faith; it acts as a perspective on his identification with spiritual progress, and therefore on the immediacy of his dramatised conception of a Christian identity which is linked to advancement and refinement of the soul. Other poems, such as 'Caliban Upon Setebos' which directly follows 'A Death in the Desert' in *Dramatis Personae*, or 'Mr Sludge' later in the same volume, employ moments of remembered experience as contributions to what is an act of histrionic immediacy, and retrospective analysis may itself become a dramatised performance as it is for the three protagonists in *The Ring and the Book*.

This dramatically based model of man as verbal artifice needs again to be distinguished from interpretations which take a solely role-playing view of personality, where the only reality is the self as mask. To argue that Browning regarded personality as a regression of masks is to make the self merely a reaction to social requirements,[3] neglecting the realities of feeling and promptings of personal desire which lie behind dramatised surfaces. Most significantly, such a view ignores the crucial function of self-awareness in the monologues, the spectator element which suggests a self which is separate from the mask or another level of consciousness reacting to the social role, aware of its function. There are poems where characters define themselves in terms of a public role and in those poems the power of a publicly provided image to govern behaviour or shape a persona is clearly seen. 'Fra Lippo Lippi', 'Bishop Blougram's Apology' and 'Mr Sludge, "the Medium"' are examples, but in each instance there is also the awareness of a self detached from the mask. Fra Lippo Lippi struggles with feelings and perceptions which are at odds with what is expected of him, Bishop Blougram matches his nature with his role, but he can only develop the argument through a sense of the distinction between the two, and Sludge claims a self which is separate from his public function. In a different example taken from *Pippa Passes*, Sebald through murdering Luca has enacted the role of a passionate lover which was encouraged in him by Ottima, but then he reacts in horror when he realises that the idealised mask became transformed through its performance into the shape of a mere 'cut-throat'. Often in the monologues the portrayal of physical sensation is substantive and rich – 'Caliban Upon Setebos' is an obvious example – and yet of far more poetic significance than the quality of the imagery is the interpretation of that sensation, not the reaction to stimulus but its accommodation by the speaker into a pattern of understanding, and, further, how that act of interpretation generates another level of awareness which is conscious of its own process – although not necessarily conscious of its meaning or potential irony.

At the same time this awareness of another self distinct from the public performer does not mean that this separate self is the 'real' person. While the potential split between self and role is exploited by Mr Sludge and Count Guido as they attempt to avoid responsibility for their public actions, their monologues also suggest the irony that this assumed dualism of perception and function is essentially the monism of reflexive consciousness. That is the point, for instance, of the way they are shown to be victims of their own conceptions, whereby their sense of detachment from the acted masks of medium, eldest son or cuckolded husband simply leaves them feeling frustrated and bitter. There is a similar point in *Fifine at the Fair*, when Juan's argument that the real self is a metaphysical illusion, existing in a dualistic relationship with the flesh that feels, is undermined by his dependence on 'touch' for confirmation of his existence. What Browning seems to portray is a paradox of self-consciousness in so far as the implicit separation of identity into self and consciousness of self is simply an illusion necessary to the function of self-awareness, and that function is important, for self-awareness is a crucial component of self-realisation.

Fundamental then to the nature of personality in the monologues is an act of self-reflexiveness, the projection of a self-image which is both speculative and specular. This image may represent an ambiguous blend of potential for fulfilment and mirroring of actuality, but without a dramatised self there can be no sense of conscious identity, since no self to be conscious of. Alternatively, without self-mirroring there may be character in terms of an unconscious puppet of unknown forces, or the one-dimensional persona of simple lyricism, lacking in any intrinsically dramatic content. But the feature of Browning's monologues is that they do involve this dimension of implicit self-scrutiny. Even the Pope in *The Ring and the Book* performs his act of judgement before himself, addressing his monologue to his secular self, and in *Prince Hohenstiel-Schwangau* the speaker as spectator is taken to its ultimate extreme when the Prince imagines his own auditor, a feature which is not revealed until the end of the poem, indicating the way most auditors might as well have been imagined, in so far as they represent some facet of the speaker's identity. The dramatised self is therefore central and it functions psychologically as a fiction which is the means of substantiating existence as an individual. Any active, perceiving subject depends for its existence on a relationship with an identifiable object, just as the subject of a sentence is defined through its function in relationship to a predicate. In dramatising themselves, the monologuists therefore make the self an object; then, through being 'experienced' in its making and in its acting, that dramatised self establishes in turn the impression of a self as the experiencing subject. Characters in monologues thus exist as the objects of their own imagination and this interplay of fictive object and subjective awareness forms an interdependent co-existence, where the illusion of an experiencing consciousness generates the reality of individual perception. The circular process of this linguistic flux is the source of self-consciousness and self-conception, both necessary illusions for the survival of an independent identity.

Also, in this constant round of solipsistic reflexiveness, Browning is obviously exploring different levels of awareness, so that the quality of the dramatised persona may be manipulated or tested in varying degrees of diffuseness or complexity, according to public demand or private need. While no one act is of necessity the real self, some characters such as the Duke of Ferrara define their nature by identifying totally with the enacted mask; others such as Andrea del Sarto struggle with more difficulty to establish some pattern or principle of unity. However, as Browning continues to experiment with the monologue form, generally expanding its length as he moves from *Men and Women* through to *Prince Hohenstiel-Schwangau* and *Fifine at the Fair*, he seems increasingly to question whether personality exists as anything other than a shifting series of dramatic hypotheses, unified only by a self-perpetuating consciousness.

Poetry and psychology unite, of course, in language. It is a truism in poetry to point to the dependency on words, but the kind of experience represented in the monologues is essentially verbal: persuasion, justification, interpretation. Without language these dramas could barely exist, except as a few superficial or trivialising gestures, and that is not always the case in literature. The dramatic action of this poetry is to be found, therefore, as I have been suggesting throughout, in the way language may be used to develop personal realities, in the way language and identity are interrelated. There is a psychological significance, for example, in the very act of declaring, so that what may seem mere assertiveness – Johannes Agricola's 'I intend to get to God' or Ben Ezra's 'Grow old along with me' – is also an attempt to rescue life from confusion through verbal firmness. It is language which allows the propagation of a personal 'myth', a fiction of existence which a speaker may recognise as his own, and language therefore which fixes perceptions into a system of understanding. The building of a plot of existence, the establishing of a pattern of relationships through narrative, is a verbally derived sense of meaningfulness. Nor should the abstractions of language mislead about the force of identity. While the self as a centre of experience may be an illusion, that illusion is very much a reality to the individual concerned. Indeed, it is the strength of conviction about that reality which makes the created mask potentially dangerous, as can be seen in 'My Last Duchess', 'Porphyria's Lover' and *The Ring and the Book*. The mask may be in itself merely a verbal fiction, but in its function it has a power of manifestation which must be acknowledged. Browning is always quite clear about the ability of fiction to initiate and influence real action: in *Red Cotton Night-Cap Country* Léonce Miranda jumps to his death through believing in the literalness of symbolic meaning.

However, while dramatising the histrionic acts which are

conceived in language allows Browning to posit the freedom of creative potential and to suggest the often overwhelming multitudinousness and vitality of human experience, the formulations of language may impose constraint as much as urge release. The puzzle of self-made labyrinths is a threat as well as an inspiration. Ultimately, then, Browning's perception of man as verbal actor is a perception of ambiguities, and the monologues convey less a consistent theory of personality than an implicit scepticism which observes the many ironies of human consciousness. Morse Peckham's comment which I quoted earlier, for instance, that to Browning character was 'self-conception as self-deception for the sake of arriving at a strategy for action' is more the observation of a psychological irony than a full definition of personality. Still, in the mimetic function of the poems, these ironies generally centre, as Peckham implies, on the ambiguous achievements of consciousness. Through the fictions of possibility which imagination may project, for instance, men agonise over a separation of knowing from being: 'How profitless to know', cries Andrea; and 'Fra Lippo Lippi', 'Cleon' and 'Too Late' all portray varying degrees of frustration and torment over a split between consciousness of potential and the limits of the actual. Histrionic acts can be both self-creative and self-destructive: for Fra Lippo Lippi they sustain a dynamic multifacetedness, but for Sludge and Guido, while apparently providing the freedom of creative fulfilment, they lead instead to an ironic dissolution of identity. In the development of self-realisation, then, the fictions of the mind are ambiguous and yet indispensable: self-consciousness is necessary in order to know what the self is, but that very knowledge leads to self-imprisonment or stasis as much as to self-fulfilment or growth. As St John argues in 'A Death in the Desert', without the fictions of conception and of consciousness there can be no goal and no striving, no self and no identity; but with such fictions there can be self-deception, inhibition and solipsism, a psychological enclosure within a self-defined pattern. Furthermore that prison may, ironically, be the very basis of identity, as it is for instance in 'Andrea del Sarto'.

The recognition of entrapment also forms the climax of 'Childe Roland to the Dark Tower Came', a poem which provides a focus for all I have been arguing. At the point when Roland's progress is thwarted and he is about to give up his quest 'one time more', he hears 'a click / As when a trap shuts' and immediately realises his plight: 'You're inside the den!' (st. xxix). In a sense this is no more than he expected, since he has assumed the attitude of victim from the outset. He presumes that the 'hoary cripple' who directs him, suppressing ill-concealed glee at gaining 'one more victim', was there to 'ensnare' him (sts. i–ii); and as he enters the new path, the day casts one last light 'to see the plain catch its estray' (st. viii). Such conceptions seem to be part of an attempt to express his sense that what occurs is not of his volition, that events are the product of some outwardly determined force. He continues because there is no choice: once he enters the plain, the road behind disappears and so 'nought else remained to do' (st. ix). Later, when the mountains appeared, they had 'stolen' into view, and it seemed that 'some trick' had happened 'to' him (st. xxix). Also, it is not so much the external phenomenon which is observed but its effect upon himself. The transformation of the plain, for instance, is registered as an altered consciousness: 'aware I somehow grew . . . the plain had given place / All round to mountains' (st. xxviii). The sudden appearance of the hills has no obvious or normal explanation, but it is nevertheless a reality of his experience, something which is happening to *him*. He seems to be one of nature's 'prisoners' who can only be set free by 'the last Judgement's fire' (st. xi); therefore all he can do is acquiesce in the cripple's directions (st. iii) and hope to fulfil the prophecies of his failure, to conform to expectations (sts. iv–vii).

But if Roland is the victim of some malevolent fate, it is his own consciousness which makes it seem so. He has no evidence for such a conception other than his own efforts to understand an otherwise meaningless landscape: as several critics have observed, his use of similes makes it clear that most of the images which characterise his journey are the result of Roland's own speculations.[4] He records how things appear to him, not as an imposition from without, but as a projection from within: among others, leprosy, the serpent, 'the fiend's glowing hoof', a 'dead man's cheek', the water-rat, toads, wild cats and boils do not exist in the literal landscape, being hypothetical horrors, products of his imagination. The dream-like strangeness of the world he travels through increasingly challenges any normal pattern of understanding, and his responses to that challenge increasingly remove him from the conventions of emotional and moral reassurance. Apparently 'all agree', for instance, that the cripple's directions are correct (st. iii), but Roland's mistrust and dislike, supported only by the negative affirmation of his own rhetorical questions (st. ii), effectively deny him the comfort

of that general acceptance. He is cut off also from either pride or
hope (st. iii) and when he enters the plain the security of the 'safe'
road disappears. When he seeks inspiration from the past, he is
reminded that Cuthbert and Giles were both found wanting, so that
the old values fail, old models for behaviour are discredited, leaving
him with only the immediacy of his journey: 'Better this present
than a past like that' (st. xviii). As the supports of social convention
are stripped away and nature is found to be barren, inhospitable
and indifferent, unable to act for itself, all comes to focus on Roland
himself and his own resources. He is isolated within his own
experience, and as details appear which have no logic to them – the
marks on the ground, for instance, with 'No foot-print' leading
away – Roland's experience is characterised more and more by his
own speculation. He is placed therefore in the situation which is so
typical of Browning's monologues of an ironic conflict between his
sense of a fate, some 'trick / Of mischief', imposing itself from
without, and the unacknowledged projection of his own interpretations from within. Roland's consciousness is the unifying focus for
this ironic ambiguity, and therefore what he feels as an impelling
fate could just as easily be his own unconscious desire for self-
discovery and meaningfulness.

The realisation that he is caught 'inside the den' marks finally a
dramatic shift in awareness, for it is then that Roland discovers the
tower and with it an ambiguous end to his journey. There is no
glorious celebration of the quester's success, no bestowing of reward
and meaning; instead, there is the ugliness and ignominy of a 'round
squat turret, blind as the fool's heart'. He discovers an inglorious
end, for in the light of the 'dying sunset' he observes the reflexive
vision of himself as the hunted:

> The hills, like giants at a hunting, lay,
> Chin upon hand, to see the game at bay, –
>   'Now stab and end the creature – to the heft!'   (st. xxxii)

As the last light shone on this scene, the names of past adventurers,
lost peers, rung in his ears, revealing at last his link with the past –
each quester is 'lost'. The vision of his predecessors then merges into
an aesthetic form which completes the image, the 'living frame'
which surrounds experience, circumscribing it, defining its limits
and therefore its end. Yet despite the anticipated destruction,
Roland announces his presence, dauntlessly blows his 'slug-horn',

asserting himself in a way that he did not do earlier when his response was to acquiesce, for in this final scene Roland confronts himself. As the object of his quest, the tower was the organising centre or defining principle for his existence, and in arriving at that centre he has reached the core of self, what Isobel Armstrong has called 'that irreducible nub of being which we irrationally intuit and which enables us to feel that we are uniquely "I"'.[5] This climax of discovery is conceived as in the fire of revelation: 'Burningly' it came upon him (st. xxx), the sunset 'kindled' its last ray (st. xxxii), and he saw his peers 'in a sheet of flame' (st. xxxiv). Fire, like the fire of Judgement which will set nature's prisoners free (st. xi), is a process of both transformation and consumption, so that Roland's moment of self-discovery is a moment of self-destruction:

> The tempest's mocking elf
> Points to the shipman thus the unseen shelf
> He strikes on, only when the timbers start.   (st. xxxi)

As his predecessors gathered to view 'the last' of him, Roland 'saw' and 'knew' them, and in that knowledge his assertion of independence merges into his unity and identity with them. The poem ends thus in an immolation which is the paradox of self-recognition that is self-dissolution.

The quest is subjectively conceived and finally self-centred in its design. While Roland apparently gives purpose to his life by carrying on against a malign fate and the promise of failure, he feels he has no choice and so can hardly be credited with purposeful will. Man seeks a cause without, following the forces of an impelling universe, only to be faced with the irony that they lead back to himself as their focus. In seeking in the tower an external object as the goal of experience, Roland discovers instead the self as a subject which is the centre of experience, and this is an irony which makes the poem, like so much of Browning's work, at once a fulfilment and a betrayal of the Romantic mythos of salvation through experience. In attempting to actualise the paradox of meaningful action in a meaningless wasteland, Roland may discover the nub of self, the ugly uniqueness 'without a counterpart / In the whole world' which is the self-justifying reality, but that is a pyrrhic victory, for meaning is only what he provides for himself. All he can do is proclaim his existence, since anything more is but a fiction of consciousness. Thus the poem is essentially the vision of a man who finally realises that he is imprisoned within consciousness. Roland is caught within his own quest, in the sense of things happening to him, of being the prey, the content of 'one more picture', and all he can discover through the awareness of this trap is his own end, for only in the fire of transformation is there release from consciousness and such a release is synonymous with death. If consciousness is the basis of self-definition then transcendence of consciousness must mean the dissolution of identity. To know the self in this way, to recognise that the object and subject of experience fuse into one all-embracing unity, is to complete a circularity of awareness which is both a definition of identity and an end to the process of existence. Perhaps Roland could begin again, pursue another goal, define another self: thus re-enact the punishment of Sisyphus, remain obedient to the impossible demands of the nymph of self-conception, like the speaker in 'Nympholeptos', Browning's 'later poem about the repetitions of entrapment.

What I have just written is an account of the poem which treats it as Harold Bloom does in *The Ringers in the Tower*, as 'a Borges parable of self-entrapment',[6] for with this focus it may be seen as a quintessential Browning poem, despite the way it differs from more orthodox monologues in situation and method of expression. There is not the particularity of character which features in many monologues, but there is a distillation of experience which makes it both the record of a particular perspective and a representation of the universal, the pattern of all human consciousness. In the few attempts to express a sequence of causation – 'So . . . I turned from him'; 'For mark!'; 'For, looking up . . .' – is the effort to understand experience through narrating it, and in thrusting the self onwards in the journey is the commitment of a persona to an action through which it may realise its place in the world. As the speaker becomes increasingly isolated amidst his own subjectivity, he undertakes the quest of all monologuists – to define some principle of reality amidst an indeterminate mixture of sensation and hypothesis, to discover the nub of self when the support of social convention and public artifice falls away. Above all, in reaching the tower Roland dramatises the predicament of all consciousness, for when he confronts the self as a product of experience, he discovers not an independent object, but the ambiguity of a self-reflexive subject. The effect of immediacy, an illusion that the journey occurs now despite the past tense narration, tends to minimise his sense of continuing consciousness and render his perspective the more fragmented: he is merely a series of observations and subjectively speculative images, passing data of the merely picaresque character, Hume's changing impressions with only memory to forge a link between them. Yet even memory is not very significant here and it is in the transformation of consciousness when it realises its self-reflexive action that identity is attained. This is the success of embodying the unity of individual awareness, incarnating the self, though it is success characterised by irony, like that in most of Browning's monologues. It is through this penetration to the grounds of individual being, to the centremost paradoxes of identity, that Browning creates some of the most refined moments of psychological ambiguity in English literature.

Notes

CHAPTER I   THE REPUDIATION OF EXPERIENCE

1. P. B. Shelley, 'A defence of poetry', in H. F. B. Brett-Smith (ed.), *Peacock's Four Ages of Poetry, Shelley's Defence of Poetry, Browning's Essay on Shelley* (Oxford: Blackwell, 1947) p. 56.
2. For the movement from lyric to dramatic poetry, see Earl R. Wasserman, *The Subtler Language* (Baltimore: The Johns Hopkins Press, 1959); and Robert Langbaum, *The Poetry of Experience* (1957; New York: Norton, 1963); for Shelley's suggestion that poetic language orders the world, see Robert Scholes, *Structuralism in Literature* (New Haven: Yale University Press, 1974) pp. 171–5.
3. 'Dejection: An Ode', *In Memoriam*, lyric CXXIII.
4. Northrop Frye, 'Expanding eyes', *Critical Inquiry*, 2 (Winter 1975) 211.
5. R. Browning, 'An essay on Percy Bysshe Shelley', in *Peacock's Four Ages . . .*, p. 67.
6. Frye, pp. 211–12.
7. Langbaum, p. 11.
8. Langbaum also says that the authority of the particular perspective in a romantic poem is 'reinforced by the autobiographical connection . . . by the identification of the speaker as Wordsworth or Coleridge' (p. 48), but such a connection is not to be made in Browning's monologues.
9. Norman N. Holland, 'Literary interpretation and three phases of psychoanalysis', *Critical Inquiry*, 3 (Winter 1976) 232.
10. Cf. the physicist Heisenberg: 'For the sciences of nature, the subject matter of research is no longer nature in itself, but nature subjected to human questioning, and to this extent man, once again, meets only with himself.' Quoted in Aldous Huxley, *Literature and Science* (Chatto & Windus, 1963) p. 65.
11. Philip Drew, *The Poetry of Browning* (London: Methuen, 1970) p. 26.
12. Ross Wetzsteon, 'Nabokov as teacher', in Alfred Appel, Jr. and Charles Newman (eds.), *Nabokov* (London: Weidenfeld & Nicolson, 1971) pp. 242–3.
13. See, e.g., Eugene Donato, 'The two languages of criticism', in Richard Macksey and Eugene Donato (eds.), *The Structuralist Controversy*, (Baltimore: The Johns Hopkins University Press, 1972) p. 96; and Claude Lévi-Strauss, *Myth and Meaning* (London: Routledge & Kegan Paul, 1978): ' "to mean" means the ability of any kind of data to be translated in a different language. I do not mean a different language like French or German, but different words on a different level' (p. 12).
14. T. S. Eliot, 'Hamlet', *Selected Essays*, 3rd edn (London: Faber, 1972) p. 145.
15. Betty S. Flowers, *Browning and the Modern Tradition* (London: Macmillan, 1976) pp. 107, 115; Morse Peckham, 'Personality and the mask of knowledge', in *Victorian Revolutionaries* (New York: Braziller, 1970) pp. 84–129.

16. This is the limitation of the approach taken by Robert F. Garratt, 'Browning's dramatic monologue: the strategy of the double mask', *Victorian Poetry*, 11 (1973) 115–25.
17. Alan Sinfield, *Dramatic Monologue* (London: Methuen, 1977) p. 64.
18. Peckham, p. 117.

CHAPTER 2 'GOD A TAME CONFEDERATE': IRONY IN *PIPPA PASSES*

1. In my attention to the reader's experience, I adhere to the now well-established practice of treating *Pippa Passes* as a play to be read rather than performed. Browning in 1849 subtitled the work 'A Drama', leaving his intention, probably deliberately, ambivalent.
2. See, e.g., Robert Langbaum, Philip Drew, and John Killham, 'Browning's "modernity": *The Ring and the Book*, and relativism', in Isobel Armstrong (ed.), *The Major Victorian Poets: Reconsiderations* (London: Routledge & Kegan Paul, 1969) pp. 153–75, particularly p. 174, n. 13.
3. It should be noted that my discussion is based on the final version of the play as edited by Ian Jack, since several studies by critics concerned with Browning's development have focused on the first edition (1841). Browning made extensive changes for the 1849 collected edition where he clarified his intentions, elaborating notably the psychology of Pippa and the responses of Jules and Luigi to her songs. The alterations are frequently important to my argument and in particular this quotation from Phene's speech was an addition to the 1849 text.
4. The first student says Phene is 'fourteen years old at farthest' (p. 332), and Betty Senescu, in 'Another Pippa', *Victorian Newsletter*, 33 (1968) 8–12, has shown that Pippa is 'about fourteen' (p. 9).
5. Margaret Eleanor (Glen) Cook, 'The meaning and structure of *Pippa Passes*', *University of Toronto Quarterly*, XXIV (July 1955) 426.
6. Cook, p. 426.
7. Mrs Cook suggests that Browning's 'use of the word "puppets" is unfortunate' (p. 413), but I regard the word as deliberate. For evidence that Browning knew of its significance both before and after *Pippa Passes*, see Dale Kramer, 'Character and theme in *Pippa Passes*', *Victorian Poetry*, 2 (1964) 243, n. 5.
8. The selfishness in each incident has been observed by Kramer (pp. 241–9), who has also anticipated my previous point that the Monsignor 'is reserving judgement on whether to raise Pippa to her rightful place' (p. 248).
9. Roma King, *The Focusing Artifice* (Ohio University Press, 1968) p. 48.
10. King, p. 51; Jacob Korg, 'A reading of *Pippa Passes*', *Victorian Poetry*, 6 (1968) 5–19.
11. Browning's skilful presentation of the tension at this point is shown further by the way the Intendant is allowed to capitalise on his coup through matching the Monsignor's verbal agility, mockingly repeating the Bishop's liturgical 'howsoever, wheresoever, and whensoever', and exercising a deft pun on 'father' (IV, p. 357).
12. This point is supported by Browning's removal, in 1849, of a line which, given to the Bishop immediately before Pippa's song, would have indicated a growing acceptance of Maffeo's claim: 'Why, if she sings, one might . . .'

13. I must acknowledge Jacob Korg's point that the Bishop's '*Miserere mei Domine*' is evidence, however slight, for his remorse (p. 17). Professor Korg, though, does not consider the Monsignor's indecision about Maffeo, and what the Bishop asks mercy *for* seems to me entirely ambiguous.
14. Peckham, p. 117.
15. That Pippa is not a waif-like model of angelic virtue has been documented by Kramer (pp. 241–5) and Senescu (pp. 8–12).
16. W. David Shaw, *The Dialectical Temper* (Cornell University Press, 1968) pp. 46–53.
17. Kramer, p. 243.
18. Shaw, p. 47.
19. See Thomas J. Collins, *Robert Browning's Moral-Aesthetic Theory, 1833–1855* (University of Nebraska Press, 1967), for the view that Pippa, as an 'ideal poet-figure', is 'a regression to the uncomplicated vision of youth' (p. 85).
20. See also Senescu: Pippa 'resorts to reciting a hymn and getting what solace she can from that' (p. 11).
21. For Browning's increasing stimulation of the reader's 'co-operating fancy', see Donald S. Hair, *Browning's Experiments with Genre* (Edinburgh: Oliver & Boyd, 1972) p. 26 and *passim*.
22. Northrop Frye, *Anatomy of Criticism* (New York: Atheneum, 1967) p. 214. Roma King observes that the play's movement is 'continuous and circular rather than horizontal' (p. 53).

CHAPTER 3   THE DRAMA OF SELF-CONCEPTION

1. See, e.g., Shaw, pp. 92–104; and Flowers, p. 106. Several of my comments on the Duke have been influenced by Shaw in particular.
2. Cf. Flowers, p. 106.
3. Michael H. Bright makes a similar suggestion about ll. 41–9, that they betray 'a grappling with painful truth', in 'Browning's "Pictor Ignotus": an interpretation', *Studies in Browning and His Circle*, 4 (1976) 58.
4. I assume the woman is present, although the image of the hiding-place in the last stanza may suggest otherwise.
5. For further suggestions about role-playing in Browning's love poems, see Isobel Armstrong, 'Browning and the Victorian poetry of sexual love', in Isobel Armstrong (ed.), *Robert Browning* (London: Bell, 1974), particularly pp. 288–9.
6. Park Honan, *Browning's Characters* (New Haven: Yale University Press, 1961) pp. 161–5.
7. See Philip Drew, p. 31.
8. Cf. Roma King: 'Lippo is unable to escape entirely the spiritual and artistic stereotypes which the external world presents for his emulation' (p. 105).
9. King, p. 106.
10. For an account of previous views and a thorough analysis of the poem's logic, see Drew, pp. 122–42.
11. Shaw, pp. 211–12.
12. See also Drew, p. 142.

13. A point made by Arnold Shapiro in 'A new (old) reading of Bishop Blougram's apology: the problem of the dramatic monologue', *Victorian Poetry*, 10 (1972) 243–56; cf. Isobel Armstrong, 'Browning and the "Grotesque" style', in *The Major Victorian Poets*: 'the emotional and moral feeling from which [Blougram] creates his structure of the world is inadequate' (p. 117).
14. Honan, pp. 156–7; Fred Kaplan, *Miracles of Rare Device* (Detroit: Wayne State University Press, 1972) p. 105.
15. A point made by Kaplan, p. 109.
16. See Langbaum, p. 154.
17. The exceptions are Robert L. Kelly, 'Dactyls and curlews: satire in "A Grammarian's Funeral"', *Victorian Poetry*, 5 (1967) 105–12, and David Shaw, pp. 81–6, who both recognise the speaker's viewpoint.
18. C. C. Clarke, 'Humor and wit in "Childe Roland"', *Modern Language Quarterly*, 23 (1962) 324.
19. The phrase is from the *Aeneid*, and I take the translation from F. B. Pinion's notes to *Dramatis Personae* (London: Collins, 1969) p. 178.
20. This point has been made previously by David Shaw: 'the dialectician becomes increasingly the object of his own irony' (p. 138).

CHAPTER 4   THE FUNCTION OF ILLUSION

1. David Shaw, p. 120.
2. Arnold Shapiro, 'Browning's psalm of hate: "Caliban Upon Setebos", Psalm 50, and *The Tempest*', *Papers on Language and Literature*, 8 (1972) pp. 56, 58, 62.
3. Shaw, p. 199.
4. For this point see Shapiro on the relationship with Psalm 50.
5. Both Arnold Shapiro, 'Caliban' (p. 59), and E. K. Brown, 'The first person in "Caliban Upon Setebos"', *Modern Language Notes*, 66 (June 1951) 392–5, observe this equation. See also Thomas P. Wolfe's article, 'Browning's comic magician: Caliban's psychology and the reader's', *Studies in Browning and His Circle*, 6 (Fall 1978) 7–24: 'Caliban unconsciously (or unselfconsciously) projects his own inner life onto Setebos, and then proceeds to discover in himself those qualities that have now become attributes of God' (p. 15).
6. See Shapiro, 'Caliban', pp. 56, 60.
7. Caliban's faulty logic is pointed out by Shapiro: 'How can he "vex" if no one overhears?' ('Caliban', p. 50). See also Wolfe, pp. 11–12.
8. E. K. Brown shows how each item in Caliban's final list is less than he promised (p. 395, n. 8).
9. John Howard has argued that there is no specific object of satire: 'Caliban's mind', *Victorian Poetry*, 1 (1963) 249–57.
10. See also Thomas Wolfe: 'I do not think anyone can properly read the poem without discovering himself to be an object of its ridicule' (p. 18). I read Professor Wolfe's essay after I had written this account, but clearly we have arrived at similar conclusions.
11. Cf. David Shaw: 'Browning is trying to narrate a medieval mystery story from the point of view of the guilty person' (p. 72).

CHAPTER 5   HISTRIONIC ACTION IN *THE RING AND THE BOOK*

1. Quotations from *The Ring and the Book* are from *The Poetical Works of Robert Browning*, vols VIII, IX, X (London: Smith, Elder, 1889), and references are to book and line number within the poem itself; this edition numbers the half-lines.
2. J. Hillis Miller, *The Form of Victorian Fiction* (Notre Dame: University of Notre Dame Press, 1968), pp. 2, 5.
3. Charles Edwin Nelson, 'Role-playing in *The Ring and the Book*', *Victorian Poetry*, 4 (1966) 94.
4. Mary Rose Sullivan, *Browning's Voices in 'The Ring and the Book'* (University of Toronto Press, 1969) p. 206n.
5. See also Morse Peckham, who has already suggested that Guido's wolf-image is 'a rationalising strategy to provide himself with self-respect', and that Guido 'reveals himself as merely an organism struggling only for continued existence' (*Victorian Revolutionaries*, p. 94). I do not agree, however, that 'Guido can maintain no mask', for in using the word 'murder' he still dramatises himself as a victim of authority.
6. See, e.g., Robert Langbaum, 'Browning and the question of myth', in *The Modern Spirit* (New York: Oxford University Press, 1970).
7. For the poet's acknowledgements of his own subjectivity, see also Morse Peckham, 'Historiography and *The Ring and the Book*', *Victorian Poetry*, 6 (1968) 243–57.
8. Langbaum, 'Browning and the question of myth', p. 84.
9. Shaw, pp. 298–9.
10. John Killham, p. 170.

CHAPTER 6   EXPERIENCE AS PAGEANT: SUBJECTIVISM IN *FIFINE AT THE FAIR*

1. *Fifine at the Fair*, section I, in *The Poetical Works of Robert Browning*, vol. XI (London: Smith, Elder, 1889) p. 221. All quotations are from this edition; future references will be documented internally by section number.
2. Fire comes to symbolise essence in the poem: the 'Self-vindicating flash' which may be elicited from each man and woman (XXIX), the soul's 'touch of God's own flame' (LXVII), the 'electric snap and spark' which prove 'there's fire and life and truth' in the world (XCI).
3. 'Soul's imaginings' replaces the first edition (1872) version of 'mere imaginings'. It is a significant alteration since Juan asserts the value of these imaginings and would not want to regard them as 'mere'.
4. For the relationship between these questions and Walter Pater's ideas, see Philip Drew, pp. 304–7.
5. See Drew, p. 308.
6. See also Drew's comments about the relevance of Schumann's *Carnaval* (Drew, p. 314, n. 1).
7. Philip Drew observes two points which suggest to him that Juan's swimming analogy is sophistical: 'First the argument is put forward to convince Elvire that Don Juan has no personal interest in Fifine, whereas the end of the poem shows this to be false. Secondly the argument is used by Juan to justify a minor

intrigue, a dabbling in deceit, which is at variance with the profound scrutiny of man's place in the world which he undertakes in the rest of the poem' (Drew, p. 312). It can be said, however, that Juan develops the analogy to convince Elvire that he can handle the dalliance with Fifine appropriately, that he will not treat Fifine as 'true' in any deep sense. Also, since deception is intrinsic to Juan's scrutiny of man throughout the poem, his concern with falsehood here is not a parenthetical aside. Nor is Fifine 'a minor intrigue' in terms of his metaphysical argument: she and Elvire embody the polarities in his personality, which has been observed by Roma King (p. 184).

8. King, p. 172. This search is also emphasised by Drew, pp. 308–20.
9. Shaw, p. 104.
10. Critics have generally regarded Juan's arguments as a mixture of truth and falsehood. However, what in the poem informs the reader of Juan's casuistry has always been problematic and recent discussions by King, Ryals and Drew emphasise the difficulty. See particularly Drew's comment on casuistry, p. 313, n. 1.
11. Drew, p. 320.

CHAPTER 7   THE SELF AS SUBJECT

1. Morse Peckham, *Victorian Revolutionaries*, p. 98. For more general accounts of personality in literature, see Robert Langbaum, *The Mysteries of Identity* (New York: Oxford University Press, 1977); Alan Kennedy, *The Protean Self* (London: Macmillan, 1974); and Patricia M. Spacks, *Imagining a Self* (Harvard University Press, 1976).
2. For this point, see Langbaum, particularly 'Wordsworth: the self as process' in *The Mysteries of Identity*, and Spacks.
3. See, e.g., Peckham, *Victorian Revolutionaries*, p. 92.
4. The point is clearly established by David Shaw, p. 128; see also Eugene R. Kintgen, 'Childe Roland and the perversity of the mind', *Victorian Poetry*, 4 (1966) 253–8, and Philip Drew, ' "Childe Roland" and the urban wilderness', *Browning Society Notes*, 8 (1978) 19–22.
5. Isobel Armstrong, 'The Brownings', in Arthur Pollard (ed.), *The Victorians* (London: Sphere Books, 1970) p. 301.
6. Harold Bloom, *The Ringers in the Tower* (University of Chicago Press, 1971) p. 162.

Index